Withdrawn

Fearless Female
SOLDIERS, EXPLORERS, AND AVIATORS

Mary Edwards Walker

THE ONLY FEMALE MEDAL OF HONOR RECIPIENT

ALISON GAINES

Cavendish Square
New York

Published in 2018 by Cavendish Square Publishing, LLC
243 5th Avenue, Suite 136, New York, NY 10016

Copyright © 2018 by Cavendish Square Publishing, LLC

First Edition

Website: cavendishsq.com

This publication represents the opinions and views of the author based on
his or her personal experience, knowledge, and research. The information
in this book serves as a general guide only. The author and publisher
have used their best efforts in preparing this book and disclaim liability
rising directly or indirectly from the use and application of this book.

CPSIA Compliance Information: Batch #CS17CSQ

All websites were available and accurate when this book was sent to press.

Library of Congress Cataloging-in-Publication Data

Names: Gaines, Alison.
Title: Mary Edwards Walker / Alison Gaines.
Description: New York : Cavendish Square, 2018. | Series: Fearless
female soldiers, explorers, and aviators | Includes index.
Identifiers: ISBN 9781502627452 (library bound) | ISBN 9781502627469 (ebook)
Subjects: LCSH: Walker, Mary Edwards, 1832-1919–Juvenile literature. |
Women physicians–United States–Biography–Juvenile literature. |
Suffragists–United States–Biography–Juvenile literature. | United States-
-History–Civil War, 1861-1865–Medical care–Juvenile literature. | United
States–History–Civil War, 1861-1865–Women–Juvenile literature.
Classification: LCC R154.W18 G35 2018 | DDC 610.92–dc23

Editorial Director: David McNamara
Editor: Stacy Orlando
Copy Editor: Nathan Heidelberger
Associate Art Director: Amy Greenan
Designer: Stephanie Flecha
Production Coordinator: Karol Szymczuk
Photo Research: J8 Media

Printed in the United States of America

Contents

one

Reform and Awakening

"You are full of resources; failing in one thing, you readily try another and another, till you ensure success."
—S. R. Wells

Mary Edwards Walker, an American Civil War doctor and a proponent of social change, may not be in every history book, but she was present during key turning points in the United States: not only the Civil War but also at the turn of the twentieth century. She believed change begins with the individual and did not wait for anyone else to

Opposite: After receiving her medal, Walker wore it daily.

set her ideas into motion. Many of her ideas were progressive, and some of her methods of implementing them might be considered unorthodox even by today's standards. In every step of her career, she cared more about furthering her ideals than she did about adhering to social norms. Her strong and perseverant personality was not deemed appropriate for a woman in her time; it was for these reasons, and many more, she encountered a lot of resistance. Although she did not see all of her philosophies implemented in her lifetime, she may be partly to thank for some of the changes that have taken place since her death, particularly for women.

Becoming a Doctor in the Nineteenth Century

Historians often describe the nineteenth century as a "coming of age" period for health care and medical education. By the mid-nineteenth century, medicine was moving toward institutional education—that is, education at medical colleges, rather than apprenticeships, as were popular in the past. Medical schools were opening in many states, branching out from Boston and Philadelphia, the traditional centers of such study. However, some of these new institutions offered degrees for very little study. There was great competition for students. Throughout the time that Walker was studying and practicing medicine, doctors seemed to outnumber patients—therefore, medicine was a competitive, yet not very lucrative, field.

Walker had very few role models to follow as a woman in medicine. In 1847, only a few years before Walker started medical school, the Geneva Medical College, in Geneva, New York, admitted Elizabeth Blackwell, who ended up being

In this painting by Matthijs Naiveu, a physician and surgeon practice bloodletting.

the first woman to receive a medical degree and formally practice medicine in the United States. Outside of her own family, who encouraged her to pursue a career as a doctor, Walker encountered much of the same resistance to her chosen path as Blackwell.

During the 1800s, medicine was not a unified science as it is today. In fact, different schools of thought proliferated separately from what became known as "regular" or "orthodox" medicine. This splintering is also referred to as medical sectarianism, similar to the way religious groups that strike out on their own are called **sects**. These alternative approaches to healing focused largely on natural remedies. Homeopathy discouraged large doses of any medication and drastic treatments, allowing the body to heal itself. **Hydrotherapy** focused on water therapy and rejected all drugs. Thomsonianism, widely popular in the United States at this time, directed patients toward changing their diets, taking herbs, and going to steam baths in order to increase body temperature. **Eclecticism**, as its name suggests, combined the aforementioned three, still in opposition to the mainstream medical beliefs and chemical-centered remedies. Syracuse Medical College, which Walker attended, aligned itself with eclecticism.

The sectarian "non-regular" schools also accepted female students at a time traditional medical institutions would not. Perhaps the non-mainstream beliefs about medicine allowed for open mindedness about accepting women into the field, or perhaps the gentler "natural" approach to healing was seen as more acceptable as a feminine vocation. Unfortunately, the medical community deemed these institutions less credible. This did not bode well for the few women entering the medical field at the time. There was an "othering" that made some doctors and schools seem less credible. Women physicians such as Walker had to stand up to questioning not only on the basis of gender but on the credibility of their education as well. In 1858, only about three hundred women had graduated from medical schools in the United States, compared to about eighteen thousand men. Walker was the only woman in her class when she graduated from Syracuse Medical College in 1855.

So, what were the mainstream medical beliefs as Walker was earning her degree and entering the field? One of the most widely used medical textbooks, George B. Wood's *Treatise on the Practice of Medicine*, may seem misguided or primitive to today's audience. For example, Wood asserted that malaria was caused by exposure to atmospheric impurities, such as the effluvia that wafted from human waste and other decomposing matter. He was correct in that malaria does come from external sources, but today's doctors know that it does not come from impurities in the air, but rather from a parasite that is most commonly carried by mosquitoes.

Also still popular at the time were the teachings of Benjamin Rush, who died a generation earlier, in 1813. Rush was a member of the Continental Congress and a signer of the Declaration of Independence, as well as one of America's first physicians. He was a big proponent of bloodletting, purging, and blistering to cure diseases, as he believed that all diseases resulted from one and the same cause: overstimulation of the blood vessels. He also prescribed mercury to his patients. Today, mercury is known to be so toxic that it's rarely even used in thermometers as it was traditionally used. During an outbreak of yellow fever in 1793, Rush's treatments were as widely feared as the disease itself; however, his methods were still relatively mainstream during the time of Walker's education.

It may be worth noting that we have very little record of Walker actually performing surgery—her work may have in fact more closely paralleled nursing, but it is hard to say. She certainly gained more surgical experience than she had before the war, and as we will discuss, her wartime duties may have expanded beyond medicine and into espionage.

The Burned-Over District

The Second Great Awakening is a nickname referring to the flurry of religious revivalism that happened during the late eighteenth and early nineteenth centuries. Its most active region, upstate New York, earned the nickname of "the burned-over district" because, after a while, there seemed to be no fresh souls left to convert. Oswego, New York, Walker's hometown, sat in the midst of this area.

During this time, Evangelical Methodism and Baptist denominations were the fastest growing religions in the nation. Ministers tried to gain converts through weekday meetings in schoolhouses or people's homes, as well as at larger camp meetings, at which hundreds of people would gather.

Evangelism had several traits that made it especially attractive to converts. Unlike Catholicism, it did not place importance on status or higher education. People's individual piousness held the most importance. Ordinary people were told they were just as important as the elite or wealthy. Evangelism taught that people had the ability to change their situation for the better, unlike in Calvinism, which emphasized man's depravity.

Some accounts state the Walker family attended Baptist and Methodist services on Sundays, but not much is known about the details of their beliefs. Baptist and Methodist Christian faiths believe in the teachings of the Holy Bible and differ in a few areas, like whether individuals should be baptized as infants or adults. Both of these religions still exist today; however, some movements during the Second Great Awakening did not end up lasting. Much religious and social experimentation abounded in the burned-over district, especially during the

1840s. Political scientist Michael Barkun writes of two main strands of transformationalism that occurred during this time: **millenarianism** and **utopianism**. These two schools of thought were quite distinct from each other, but both emerged from rejection of the status quo.

Millenarians believed that the end of the world, or the Second Coming of Christ, was approaching, and therefore did their best to amass as many believers as possible. The most obvious example of millenarianism was William Miller and his sect known as Millerism. Miller, a Baptist preacher, predicted that Christ's Second Coming would occur between March 21, 1843, and March 21, 1844. When his prediction failed to come true, Miller changed his prediction to the following October. Millerites called this lack of apocalypse the Great Disappointment.

At the same point in time, other individuals took an opposite, but seemingly parallel, track and started to form utopian communities. Unlike millenarians, who sought to convert as many believers as possible before the end of the world, the utopians sought to seclude themselves from society, often abiding by some very unorthodox conventions. Barkun calls the utopian communities a "combination of religious observance and social reform."

The most famous utopian community from that time was the Oneida Community, founded by John Humphrey Noyes. It started as a group of fewer than fifty people in his hometown of Putney, Vermont, and in 1848, moved to Oneida County, New York, just southeast of Oswego, Mary Edwards Walker's hometown. In pursuit of Perfectionism, the commitment to living a sin-free life, Noyes and his followers adopted a communal identity, with fluid interpersonal possessions and relationships.

The Oneida Community practiced what Noyes called "complex marriage," or nonexclusive sexual relationships. His belief was rooted in the question he asked his followers: "Is not now the time for us to commence the testimony that the Kingdom of God as come?" Sexual relations, he believed, served both a reproductive as well as an "amative" function which, to be clear, quite contradicted the mainstream beliefs at the time. Public memory of the Oneida Community mostly centers on this aspect of nonreproductive sexual partnerships, and the way a sort of marriage among everyone emerged out of that.

Oneida also turned away from other social conventions, such as wage labor, private property, the traditional family, and subordination of women. Oneida women dressed in trousers and shorter dresses. Later on, when discussing **dress reform**, Mary Walker would refer to the women of Oneida.

This mansion, built by the Oneida Community, is today a National Historic Landmark.

Civil War: The Broad Strokes

The American Civil War ended up providing the start of Walker's career in earnest. Thankfully, many written accounts and photographs survive, so these firsthand stories can help modern audiences understand how the war affected individual lives.

The war stretched from April 1861 to April 1865, when General Robert E. Lee of the **Confederacy** surrendered to General Ulysses S. Grant. Before the start of the war, Southern states began to secede from the **Union** around the time that Abraham Lincoln was elected president. In fact, he won the presidency without even appearing on the ballot in ten Southern states.

Why did the South wish to disconnect itself from the Union? For one, they saw Lincoln's campaign as a danger to the Southern way of life. He ran his 1860 campaign on the platform of stopping the spread of slavery—those who deny freedom to others, he said, did not deserve to have it themselves.

Slavery was mostly defunct in the North since the American Revolution, but it held on much more strongly in the South, since the Southern economy relied more on farming, especially of cotton. As historian Barbara J. Fields puts it, "If there was a single event that caused the war, it was the establishment of the United States in independence from Great Britain with slavery still a part of its heritage." John J. Chapman describes slavery as a "sleeping serpent," a conflict that had been present since the country created a Declaration of Independence that applied to only some of its people. Lincoln's election could be seen as the kettle of this conflict boiling over.

At the time of Lincoln's election, the Union contained thirty-three states. By the time Lincoln was inaugurated in March 1863,

Oswego County in the 1830s

Mary Edwards Walker was born during the presidency of Andrew Jackson. At the time, the United States had twenty-four official states, Missouri being the most recent addition in 1821. An era of land speculation was at its height during 1834–1836, during which time Oswego Town started to come into its own as a city. The county sat on the eastern shore of Lake Ontario, and the Oswego River ran through Oswego (closest to the lake) and down through Minetto and Fulton, other places where Mary lived, worked, and studied.

Besides all the religious and social reformism going on in the region, there was what a historian of Oswego County called "the celebrated era of speculation." In his 1877 history of the county, Critchfield Johnson looks back on a few decades prior: "Nearly all the people in the United States thought they were going to get rich at once, by the rise of land." Oswego County was no exception, and the Walkers themselves moved to buy their 33-acre (13-hectare) farm just before Mary was born.

The year 1836, unfortunately, brought a market crash, and "all the imaginary wealth of the country faded out of existence," according to Johnson. The Walkers remained on their farm, and Mary would return to take care of it in her later years. Between 1830 and 1835, the population of Oswego County increased to over eleven thousand people, but during the second half of the decade it increased less than half as much. These economic hard times may have had a hand in driving ordinary people to new religions, such as the many sects proliferating at the time, or to crusade for social reforms like Mary did.

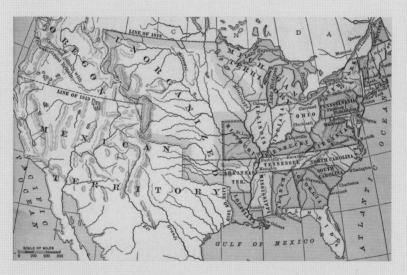

This map shows what the United States looked like in the 1830s.

seven states—South Carolina, Mississippi, Florida, Alabama, Georgia, Louisiana, and Texas—had seceded. Virginia, Tennessee, Arkansas and North Carolina followed suit after the war officially began. Soon, Jefferson Davis was elected as president of the Confederate States of America. His vice president, Alexander Stephens, believed that the foundation of the government was the fact that "the Negro is not equal to the White man."

It should be noted that neither side allowed black soldiers to enlist at first. Many people in the North, in fact, did not see this as a war over the rights of black people or as a war about ending slavery. Lincoln, despite his message during his campaign, held fast to the message that the war was against secession, not against slavery. In 1862, Congress finally passed a law allowing blacks to enlist, but it was not until 1863 that any black soldiers officially fought, and they were paid less than whites. By the end of the war, black soldiers made up 10 percent of the Union army.

The first shots of the war were fired on Fort Sumter, a man-made island in Charleston Harbor, on April 12, 1861. Union soldiers had been using the island as a base, and Confederates fired on them. The Union surrendered, and their commanding officer was taken prisoner, but it was an entirely bloodless battle, losing no one except a Confederate horse. Three days later, Lincoln called for seventy-five thousand volunteers to be soldiers for the Union army.

The attitude, for the most part, was one of excitement. Young men on both sides were eager to sign up, and the general belief was that the war wouldn't last more than ninety days. The initial major battle, called the First Battle of Bull Run by the Union, and Battle of First Manassas by the Confederacy, smashed that belief.

This is an artist's rendering of Walker tending to a wounded soldier on the battlefield

Advertised in newspapers, the battle, which took place only 20 miles (32 kilometers) from Washington, DC, drew spectators. Civilians brought picnic baskets and waited to see if they could catch a glimpse of the battle on July 21, 1861. However, once Confederate reinforcements showed up and the Union had to begin to retreat, the spectators must have realized that the spectacle was much more serious than they expected. The five thousand soldier **casualties** of the battle made it apparent that this would be no ninety-day war.

The war was mostly fought on people's farms and practically in their yards. Needless to say, soldiers weren't the only ones to feel the effects of the war. Some towns in the midpoint of the North and South, like in Virginia, changed hands many times over the years as the Union and Confederacy moved back and forth on each other.

This was the bloodiest war in American history by far. At the end of it, the number of soldier deaths is estimated to be around 660,000, possibly as high as 850,000, for both North and South combined. With civilian casualties considered, the number is over 1 million, 3 percent of the population.

Both sides of the conflict traveled and fought in **regiments** with people from the same state or even the same town, with names like "Sixth Mississippi" or "Twentieth Maine." For most soldiers, the war was the first time they'd been away from home for any period of time. A soldier's chance of dying in combat was one in sixty-five. His chance of being wounded, however, was one in ten. One in thirteen would die of disease. Doctors and nurses had their work cut out for them.

On top of causing so many fatalities, the war stretched on and strained the resources of the country to the point that many civilian communities started to run out of necessary supplies because many resources were being diverted to the war effort and because the war had disrupted regular lines of trade. During the worst parts, such as the Union army's forty-eight-day siege of Vicksburg, Mississippi, towns ran out of paper and had to print gazettes on other materials, such as wallpaper.

Both armies had to institute drafts so that they would have enough men. The South felt the deficit of men quickly. In mid-1862, Davis passed the Conscription Act. This came at a time when the earliest volunteers' enlistments were soon to be up, and the soldiers anticipated going home. However, the law stated that all enlistments were for the duration. The act was also a draft: all able-bodied white men between eighteen and thirty-five years of age were required to serve in the Confederate army for three years. Some exceptions to the draft were allowed, including anyone who owned twenty or more slaves. The Conscription Act was at odds with the very reason that the South seceded in the first place: they wanted a decentralized government. About half of the men to whom the draft applied did not sign up.

Lincoln eventually had to call for a draft to supplement Union forces as well, but it took him much longer to do so. In July 1863, he finally did. However, draftees could pay a $300 fine to get out of it or hire a substitute. The war drew severely on the population of young men in the United States, especially in the poor and middle class. Both armies desperately wanted more soldiers, but they never allowed women to enlist. However, historians have found evidence that at least 250 women disguised as men fought in the war. Women were not accepted in the military until much later, and only in limited capacities at first.

The Plight of a Yankee Woman Doctor

Mary Walker saw the beginning of the Civil War as an opportunity to practice medicine in a place where her skills were truly needed. She had her eye on a **commission** as a military surgeon. However, shortly after the fighting began, the Army Medical Department tightened its regulations and requirements for doctors with the Union army. Now, any

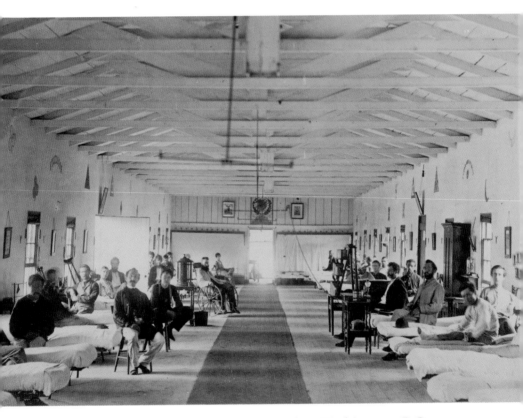

A ward in the Armory Square Hospital in Washington, DC, during the Civil War

regimental or assistant surgeon had to be first appointed by a governor, and there was no **precedent** for women as doctors. Female nurses were eventually permitted because people tended to see nursing as an acceptable vocation utilizing women's natural abilities.

Already realizing how difficult it may be to obtain a commission, Walker traveled straight to Washington, DC, to speak to the Army Medical Department in person, requesting a commission as an army surgeon. Her first request was denied. Walker then visited various hospitals in the area and found the Indiana Hospital, or the Patent Hospital, called so because it was set up in the US Patent Office. It was here she met the resident doctor, Dr. J. N. Green, working alone. Dr. Green allowed Walker to share his duties, probably because he could not refuse the help. According to Walker's correspondence, she eventually gained as much authority as Dr. Green himself. However, she left after two months, likely because she was not earning any money and not getting any closer to being a commissioned doctor. Even with a written recommendation from Dr. Green, the surgeon general refused to grant Walker a commission, and her request was denied again.

Walker spent some time in her hometown, and at the end of 1862 she returned to DC. She then traveled to find areas where her help could be of use (and possibly not refused). First, she landed in Warrenton, Virginia, tending to the soldiers of General Ambrose Burnside. Later, near Fredericksburg, Virginia, she cared for the sickest soldiers along with the managing surgeons there. These two stints in Virginia occurred adjacent to some of the bloodiest battles so far in the war, those of Antietam and Fredericksburg.

A Declaration of Sentiments

In Seneca Falls, New York, not far from the farm where Mary Walker lived with her family, the First Women's Rights Convention took place in July of 1848. Walker was a teenager at the time so she would not have attended; yet, the ideals expressed by the women at the convention aligned closely with the ideals that she lived by and fought for her whole life.

The main event of the convention was the Declaration of Sentiments, a document that garnered the signatures of sixty-eight women and thirty-two men. It mirrors some of the language of the Declaration of Independence, which the Founding Fathers used to distinguish the United States as a new nation, free of its previous colonizers. The leaders at Seneca Falls, including such noteworthy feminists as Elizabeth Cady Stanton and Lucretia Mott, likely had a deeper point when they penned their declaration to sound much like Thomas Jefferson's of 1776. By doing so, they were saying that a big change was needed and that the issue of inequality between women and men was of equal importance to the issue of the country's own independence.

Both declarations begin with the phrase "When in the course of human events," but of course differ in their content. The Declaration of Independence refers to human rights as "the separate and equal station to which the Laws of Nature and of Nature's God entitle them." The Declaration of Sentiments asserts not that "all men are created equal," but that "all men and women are created equal."

This print shows Lucretia Mott being protected from a mob that broke up a suffragettes' meeting.

The Declaration of Sentiments goes on to list ways in which women have suffered because of the established laws and societal norms. According to the declaration, men had:

- Closed off avenues of wealth and distinction to women, including higher education and most jobs.

- Required women to obey laws that they had no say in creating.

- Taken away wages and property rights, even if the women had earned them.

- Created a "false public sentiment" by maintaining two different moral codes, one for men and one for women.

- "Endeavored, in every way that he could to destroy her confidence in her own powers, to lessen her self-respect, and to make her willing to lead a dependent and abject life."

Women of the nineteenth century who crusaded for their rights are mostly remembered as suffragettes, campaigning for the right to vote. In reality, feminism meant different things to different women, just like it does today, and not everyone saw the vote as the most important goal. For Mary Walker, dress reform was of equal, if not more, importance, although she did participate in activist efforts for women's **suffrage** as well.

In the fall of 1863, Walker traveled to Chattanooga, Tennessee, where over eight thousand Union soldiers were wounded in the Battle of Chickamauga. Even though she had a letter from the assistant surgeon general recommending she be employed as a surgeon, the surgeon in charge at Chattanooga would only hire her as a nurse. While this did not satisfy Walker, she stayed for a few months, offering her services voluntarily.

By this point, Walker had grown quite frustrated. The military establishment continually accepted her voluntary help but never returned it with compensation or recognition as a commissioned officer. Walker decided to write to President Lincoln, writing about herself as "the undersigned." In the letter, Walker "begs to say to his Excellency that she has been denied a commission, solely on the ground of sex, when her services have been tested and appreciated without a commission and without compensation and she fully believes that had a man been as useful to our country as she modestly claims to have been, a star would have been taken from the National Heavens and placed upon his shoulder."

Apparently, she did not find a sympathetic supporter in Lincoln. Five days later, he wrote back, refusing her request on the grounds of not wanting to upset the authority that was in place among the military medical hierarchy.

At the beginning of the next year Dr. A. J. Rosa, a surgeon of the Fifty-Second Ohio Volunteers, died, and Mary finally triumphed in her quest to be officially employed with the Union. General George H. Thomas, whom Walker had worked with in Chattanooga, recommended her appointment in Rosa's place as a civilian contract surgeon. Her contract as acting assistant surgeon would pay her eighty dollars per month. The group was then based near Chattanooga.

Upon arriving, Walker found that most of the soldiers were in good health and in their winter quarters, unlike her previous sojourns in Warrenton and Fredericksburg. So when she was not treating the soldiers, both Union and Confederate alike, she treated Southern civilians, whose lives were also rocked by the presence of the war in their community. She delivered babies, pulled teeth, and performed many other procedures, often without payment.

Two months into her time with the Fifty-Second Ohio, in April of 1864, Walker was by herself in enemy territory and captured by Confederate soldiers, who believed her to be a spy. They took her to a political prison called Castle Thunder in Richmond, Virginia, a journey that took several days. Confederate captain Benedict J. Semmes later described her as "a thing that nothing but the debased and depraved Yankee nation could produce." The Confederates were horrified at her clothing—she was of course dressed in reform dress—and at her language. According to Semmes, she was "not good looking and of course had tongue enough for a regiment of men." Walker's time as a prisoner, which will be explored in more detail later, lasted four months, during which time she continued to refuse to dress in the traditional ladies' outfits.

Upon her release, she received $432.36 for five months of service, four of which she spent imprisoned. Still wanting a true medical department commission, Walker then confronted Major General William T. Sherman in Atlanta. He declined her request, chided her for wearing breeches, and suggested that she "imitate the example of women in hoops and petticoats, who are devoting their time to the work of nursing." Once again, Walker came up against the notion that she could be truly helpful if she would only confine herself to traditional "women's work."

The Union army would not grant Walker a commission, but they did continue her contract, which next took her to a female prison hospital in Louisville, Kentucky, where she worked as a medical officer. Walker was later put in charge of an orphans' asylum in Clarksville, Tennessee, where she was also responsible for refugee families. On June 15, 1865, a month after the war was over, Walker was transferred to Washington, DC, and her contract was terminated. This contract was the closest thing Walker achieved to an actual army commission, and during it, she spent time as a political prisoner and was chastised by one of the most important officials in the war for not dressing properly.

Walker encountered so much resistance to her desire to serve in an official capacity, even though the country was in a time of unprecedented crisis. This means that pursuing a career as a doctor, had a war not been raging, would have posed even larger challenges. Simply put, Walker was able to get away with much more than a woman physician usually could—and she knew this. Once the war ended, this leniency ended as well, and her contract was promptly terminated against her will. For the rest of her life, Walker dedicated herself to several causes, especially women's dress reform. She traveled much and gave lectures in Europe as well as in the United States about her wartime experience.

two

Her Liberal Upbringing

"You will never consent to play second, nor be held in subjection, but you must have equal rights and privileges in all things." —S. R. Wells

Few records survive from Mary Edwards Walker's childhood, so we do not know, for instance, what exactly inspired her to become a doctor, or what sparked her interest in dress reform. We can speculate that her open-minded parents and life on a farm, with many older sisters and only

Opposite: An 1855 painting of Oswego, New York, by David William Moody.

Elizabeth Smith Miller

Born before Walker, in 1822, Elizabeth Smith Miller was one of the earliest advocates of dress reform. Miller, from the same region of New York as Walker, may have received the inspiration for reform dress by the water cure practitioners in Geneva (who wore loose-fitted clothing), or from the members of the Oneida Community. Regardless of where she got the idea, her contemporaries acknowledged that she was the first woman to wear the fashion consistently. Miller and her family were supporters of women's equality as well as ending slavery. In fact, a generation before, her family's home had served as a stop on the Underground Railroad.

Miller's first cousin once removed was Elizabeth Cady Stanton, one of the core organizers of the convention in Seneca Falls. Shortly after Miller adopted the reform dress in 1851, she wore her reform dress to visit Stanton. Stanton became quite taken with the outfit once she saw it in person, and started wearing it herself. She also shared the idea with her friend Amelia Bloomer, who ran the ladies' magazine the *Lily*. When Bloomer publicized the reform dress in her magazine, the outfit became associated with her name, hence the often-used nickname "the Bloomer costume" or simply "Bloomers." However, Ms. Bloomer resented the name. It may have been through this publicity that Mary Walker first heard about the reform dress.

Miller gave an account of her experience wearing the reform dress and eventually going back to normal feminine clothes. She wrote that her husband and father supported

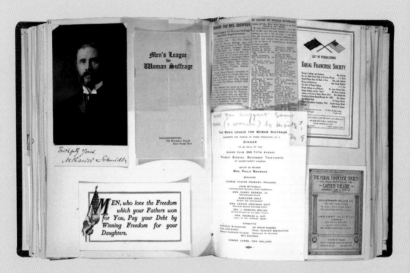

A spread from Miller's scrapbook, including a photograph of Nathaniel Schmidt, a Baptist minister and member of the New York State Women's Suffrage Association

her choice in wearing the dress, and that Elizabeth Cady Stanton had even remarked, "The question is no longer, how do you look, but woman, how do you feel?" She wrote that it made working in the garden much easier, as well as carrying children up and down stairs much safer.

However, Miller also wrote that the "Bloomers" were "a perpetual violation of my love for the beautiful." After about seven years wearing the outfit, she transitioned to longer and longer skirts, and lost the trousers. She could not quite feel comfortable in the reform dress, but she did acknowledge a hope that women would one day be able to wear clothes that were both reasonable and beautiful instead of having to choose between the two. Miller was not alone in eventually abandoning the Bloomer outfit for the more traditional one. Many other women's rights leaders stated that they appreciated its convenience, but it conflicted with either their own comfort or with others' to the point that it distracted from their activism. For Mary Edwards Walker, who never went back to traditional dress, the reform dress was inextricably tied to women's health and rights, so its abandonment by others likely seemed a huge compromise to her.

one younger brother, may have contributed to her toughness and self-confidence.

Mary's Early Years

Alvah Walker traveled a lot before he met his wife. He hailed from Greenwich, Massachusetts, originally. He became an apprenticed carpenter when he was thirteen, shortly after his father died. At the age of nineteen, he traveled westward from his hometown to Pittsburgh, then traveled south. He kept a diary during these years, and from this we know that he spent a few weeks in Louisville, Kentucky; Natchez, Mississippi; and New Orleans. Along the way, he made a living with carpentry work. While in the South, he briefly witnessed slaves laboring on a cotton plantation, which may have helped form his convictions on slavery. By this time, slavery in the North, where he and his wife had grown up, was mostly dead, so this would have been his first exposure to it.

From New Orleans, Alvah secured passage on a boat, the *Oliver*, up to Boston and then to his hometown. Upon his return, he met Vesta Whitcomb, and they married within three months. Like Alvah, Vesta came from a family that had lived in New England for generations. She had relatives who fought in the French and Indian War and the American Revolution.

Alvah and Vesta decided to move west to Kentucky, and they set out the morning after their wedding in a covered wagon. After about a week of traveling, they stopped in Otisco, New York, where Vesta's sister lived. Here, for reasons biographers cannot quite discern, the Walkers turned their wagon around and settled in the nearby brand-new town of Syracuse. The town's position on the yet-to-be-opened Erie Canal, which would offer many carpentry opportunities for Alvah, may have informed the Walkers' decision to stay.

It was a difficult first year for the newly wed Walkers. Vesta gave birth to a son, but he died within a few days. She also fell gravely ill for several weeks. Her husband, too, fell sick from complications from the measles. It was at this time Alvah became deeply interested in medicine, and he acquired and read medical books to attempt to understand his condition. He also quit the use of tobacco and alcohol. This passion for medicine, and the health of himself and his family, continued throughout his life, and would become important to Mary as well.

Over the next few years in Syracuse, Alvah and Vesta had four children, all daughters: Vesta, Aurora Borealis, Luna, and Cynthia. Ten years after establishing themselves in Syracuse, they moved to a 33-acre (13 ha) farm in Oswego Town, New York. As well as building a house and a barn for the family, Alvah erected a schoolhouse, the town's first, with the help of some neighbors. Three months after the family arrived in Oswego Town, on November 26, 1832, Mary Edwards was born. A year later, the Walkers had a son, Alvah Jr.

Farm life carried with it many responsibilities that would ordinarily fall to only the men in the family, but given the makeup of the Walker family, five girls and one boy, everyone did their share of the work. Like many families in the North, the Walkers believed in the **abolition** of slavery. Mary and her sisters were expected to do the household chores and heavy labor as well. For this reason, and because their parents (correctly) believed that tight-fitting clothing was unhealthy, the Walker girls did not wear corsets. Mary's later crusades for dress reform undoubtedly had her parents to thank.

A portrait of Amelia Bloomer on the cover of a piece of sheet music called "The Bloomer Polka"

Major Dr. William Watson, a Male Surgeon

William Watson, a twenty-five-year-old recent graduate of Lafayette College and the University of Pennsylvania, served as a surgeon with the 105th Regiment of Pennsylvania Volunteers during the Civil War. He was with them through the battles of Fredericksburg, Chancellorsville, Gettysburg, and others. He wrote frequently to his family—he had six younger sisters—and from his letters, we can see that life as a soldier was certainly rough. Watson did not, however, have to contend with people questioning his medical education or turning him down for a commission. He received his official commission from the governor of Pennsylvania in September of 1862. From the start of his involvement with the Union army, he had the rank of major.

His early letters detail the difficulties he had in setting himself up with the regiment: he arrived without a horse and was told that he needed to provide his own. His winter coat was stolen, he never seemed to have enough money, and at times, he struggled to have enough to eat.

In a letter from Gettysburg on July 7, 1863, just a few days after the bloody battle ended, Watson described his conditions:

> I am safely through the most desperate conflict I ever witnessed ... So you may know the fighting was close. I never was and never wish to be in such a shower of solid shot and shell. The house and barn occupied as a hospital were completely riddled. Of course we were compelled to fall back; in doing so a solid shot

An amputation at Gettysburg outside a medical tent in 1863

passed within a few feet of the mare's head. She threw herself flat on the ground, did not hurt me. I never had so many operations. Day before yesterday I performed fourteen amputations without leaving the table. I do not exaggerate when I say I have performed at the least calculation fifty amputations. There are so many severely wounded through the joints ... I have yet to see the first thing brought in for the comfort of the wounded. Some farmers brought in some bread which they sold for seventy-five cents a loaf. The brave army that has protected this State surely deserves better treatment.

Watson's letters illustrate the grim poverty that soldiers generally experienced. Today we might be tempted to think of the military as a well-funded, state-of-the-art institution. While the Union army was certainly innovative, it was also a poor one, and it quickly felt the need for more resources of all kinds.

Mary's parents believed that she and her sisters should have educations and careers if they so chose. Like her older sisters, Mary attended Falley Seminary, about 10 miles (16 km) from her home, during the winters from 1850 to 1852. She attended only for the winter terms because she was likely needed at home during the warmer months. Attending school only during the winter was very common in farming communities. The first term was fourteen weeks, and the second was shortened to seven, considerably less schooling than is required today owing to the work expected of the students on the farms.

After finishing school, Walker secured a teaching job in 1852 in Minetto, 5 miles (8 km) from home. By this time, she had decided to become a physician, and she saved her money from teaching to attend medical college. Higher education for women was barely existent in the 1800s, and most women's colleges were not founded until after the Civil War. Nonetheless, she ended up attending Syracuse Medical College, which had just opened the year before. She graduated in 1855, the only woman in her class.

Walker became a physician not only because she wanted to, and not only because she worked hard to do so, but equally because she was told from a young age that she could. She did not grow up believing that such a career was out of reach for her because of her gender. Unfortunately, person after person would challenge her worth as a physician throughout her life, but her parents never did.

When, as an adult, Walker published her book *Hit*, which details her opinions on many issues from dress reform to marriage to **temperance**, she dedicated it to her parents. Not much firsthand information exists about Walker's childhood, but her parents clearly had a large influence on how she moved forward with her life. Her father's liberal views on gender allowed Mary to carry herself with more confidence than she might have gained in a more conservative household.

Young Adulthood and Higher Education

Walker met her future husband at Syracuse Medical College. She and her classmate Albert Miller married after graduating in 1855. The ceremony took place at the Walker family home in Oswego. Walker showed up to the ceremony wearing trousers and a dress coat. The vow to obey her spouse was absent from the vows. Additionally, Walker never changed her name, although she occasionally signed her last name as Miller-Walker.

For several years, Miller and Walker lived together in Rome, New York, where they ran a medical practice together. However, Walker banished Miller when she found out that he had been unfaithful in 1860. Their divorce did not become final until 1869. Mary did not marry again, but she did maintain her belief that "true conjugal companionship is the greatest blessing of which mortals can conceive in this life."

Shortly after breaking things off with Miller, Walker moved offices to open her own, and she placed an ad in the local newspaper, the *Sentinel*. In an unusual move, the paper published commentary on her ad in its classified section: "As there is generally alleged to be so much rivalry and jealousy between those of the medical profession, we hardly dare to venture to give one of them a 'puff,' even by way of

Walker in an 1865 photograph. Here she wears a traditional example of the reform dress.

Hydropathic and Hygienic Institute,

15 LAIGHT STREET, NEW YORK,

R. T. TRALL, M. D., - - - Proprietor.

THIS establishment, which is pleasantly and quietly located near St John's Park, can now accommodate over ONE HUNDRED patients. Office consultations are attended to by Dr. Trall personally; and out-door practice by himself and assistants.— Competent female physicians are also provided; and particular attention is given to that class of diseases which require surgical or mechanical treatment. Patients who prefer to be in the country will be provided for at the Highland House Water-Cure, at Fishkill, N. Y., under the personal direction of Dr. O. W. May. Patients at either establishment can have the occasional advice of both physicians.

SCHOOL DEPARTMENT.

The NEW YORK HYDROPATHIC AND PHYSIOLOGICAL SCHOOL, having become a permanent institution, the regular Lecture term will hereafter commence November 1st of each year, and continue SIX MONTHS. Additional Chemical, Anatomical, Surgical and Obstetrical Apparatus has been provided; the Library has been increased; the Professorships rearranged and enlarged. Particular attention will be paid to Practical Anatomy, Dissections, and Obstetrical Demonstrations.

FACULTY:

R. T. TRALL, M. D., Institutes of Medicine, Materia Medica and Female Diseases.
G. H. TAYLOR, M. D., Chemistry, Surgery, and Obstetrics.
JAMES HAMBLETON, M. D., Anatomy, Physiology and Hygiene.
J. E. SNODGRASS, M. D., Medical Jurisprudence.
H. F. BRIGGS, M. D., Philosophy of Voice and Speech.
L. N. FOWLER, A. M., Phrenology and Mental Science.
MRS. L. F. FOWLER, M. D., Female Diseases and Obstetrics.

The design of this School is not only to qualify male and female practitioners of the Healing Art, but also to educate and send into the field of human progress, competent Health-reform Teachers and Lecturers. Ample facilities are provided for a complete and thorough medical education, and for practical instruction in all the details of Hydropathic home-practice, as well as the management of Water-Cure Establishments.

Students will have the opportunity of witnessing the treatment of almost all forms of chronic diseases in the Institution, and by visiting the cliniques and hospitals of the other Schools in the city, they will become proficient in *diagnosis*—the most important element in a physician's education, so far as success in securing public confidence is concerned—but also enabled to see the different medical systems *practically contrasted*; in other words, to witness the effects of water-treatment in contrast with the various modifications of drug treatment.

PROGRAMME OF EDUCATIONAL EXERCISES.—Usually there will be four Lectures daily, of one hour each. Half an hour, morning and evening, will be devoted to gymnastic and elocutionary exercises; and specified portions of each day will be allotted to private study, and to conversation in the class. A *clinique* will be held every Friday afternoon; and on Saturdays the students will visit the hospitals and public institutions, where a great variety of surgical operations are performed, and where almost every phase of diseased and deformed humanity can be seen.

There will be a Lyceum debate on general subjects each Wednesday evening, open to the public, and a discussion every Saturday evening on professional questions, by members of the class exclusively.

SUMMER TERM.—There will be a Summer Term of six months, from May 1st to Nov. 1st, with occasional lectures and cliniques for such students as choose to remain the year round. Tuition $50; Do. with board, $100.

R. T TRALL, M. D., Principal.

15 LAIGHT STREET, NEW YORK.

American Portrait Gallery, NY (1855)

28 N
G. New York City- Hospitals-1800s

Walker attended the New York Hygeio-Therapeutic College (originally called the Hydropathic and Hygienic Institute, a flyer for which is displayed here), in 1862, where she studied hydrotherapy.

preference over the other. Those, however, who prefer the skill of a female physician to that of the male, have now an excellent opportunity to make their choice." This comment from the newspaper seems to accept women as physicians, if only on the grounds of a patient's preference. Walker started out intending only to see women and children patients, but she occasionally treated men as well.

In 1862 Walker took a break from volunteering to attain a second medical degree from the New York Hygeio-Therapeutic College in New York City. Like Syracuse Medical College, this institution had opened just a few years prior. Unlike Syracuse, however, about half of the prior graduates of New York Hygeio-Therapeutic College were women. The college devoted itself to water therapy, or water cure, one of the medical sects that was seen as outside the medical mainstream, but at the height of popularity.

The practice believed in water-related remedies, such as baths, compresses, and wet sheets, as opposed to the harsher tactics of orthodox medicine. It privileged a moderate diet and exercise, and unlike orthodox medicine, it encouraged prevention and self-treatment. Hydrotherapy clashed not only with the conventional medical establishment but also with the current notions of femininity. Living an active lifestyle, walking several miles a day, and taking care of oneself and each other medically were not expected or approved behaviors for nineteenth-century females. Walker likely attended the New York Hygeio-Therapeutic College as a refresher course, or supplement, to her existing eclectic medical education.

Dr. Mary Walker
Army Surgeon

Medal of Honor
USA 20c

three

The Career of Miss/Doctor/ "Major" Walker

"The love for home, is the same, though you can make yourself almost at home anywhere." —S. R. Wells

Although Walker repeatedly requested employment, she was not officially connected with the Union army; she was not on the payroll and did not hold a rank. At times, her volunteer status afforded her more freedom than a soldier would have, and certainly more freedom in traveling

Opposite: In 1982, to mark the 150th anniversary of Walker's birth, the US Postal Service issued a twenty-cent stamp in her honor.

than any solitary woman would have. Soldiers also tended to view her as an all-purpose maternal figure and nurse, so she ended up performing many tasks outside of medical care. Men who needed a letter written, or who needed consolation when in a dangerous medical state, or who just needed a listening ear, would turn to Walker.

Walker's Volunteer Posts

During Walker's two months at the Indiana Hospital, she also visited the Deserters' Prison in Alexandria to hear the prisoners' stories. While the guards denied her entry at first, they let her in when she introduced herself as Dr. Walker of the Union army. After conducting interviews with some of the inmates, she concluded that some of them were wrongly imprisoned. By speaking with the War Office, she managed to secure a pardon for one boy who had walked away from his regiment to visit his dying mother. We know this from Walker's own notes on her time in the war.

While in DC attempting to gain a commission, Walker joined several benevolent projects, the most notable of which was the Women's Relief Association. Walker knew that women would often arrive in the city, looking for their wounded husbands or sons, and have trouble finding accommodations. As a volunteer, Walker could move about freely, but it was considered inappropriate for a woman to travel without an escort. If a woman arrived at a hotel or boarding house alone, she might be turned away. For this reason Walker helped form the Women's Relief Association, one of a few such organizations that sprung up during the war, that raised funds to help women find places to stay. The group had success and even convinced the chairman of the Congressional Committee for the District of Columbia to open a house for "unprotected females and children who are frequently found about on the streets of [DC] without friends, money or home." Walker also opened her own home and ran a sort of boarding house, with surplus army medical supplies on hand. Early in 1864, she withdrew from her positions in the organization and left it in the hands of others, being drawn to other matters.

In late 1862, after completing her education at New York Hygeio-Therapeutic College, Walker traveled to Virginia, again aiming to place herself where she was most needed. In Warrenton, Virginia, she assisted the troops of General Burnside, again as a volunteer. Among the soldiers she found several cases of typhoid. Medical supplies were extremely scarce. According to her notes, Walker took nightgowns from her own trunk, cut them into squares, and showed the other doctors and nurses how to apply them as bandages. Also during this stint, Walker believed that some of the wounded soldiers would receive better care in DC, and she recommended to General Burnside that they be transported there. Burnside agreed, and even charged her with accompanying the wounded on the journey.

Warrenton sits about 70 miles (113 km) away from the site of what was the bloodiest battle to date: the Battle of Antietam. The battle was fought in a cornfield near Sharpsburg, Maryland, on September 17, 1862. While it was a Union victory, it was also very costly. Walker likely saw patients that had come from the battlefield. The battle resulted in roughly 20,000 casualties including Confederate and Union troops. Of those, about 3,650 were killed in battle, and the rest were wounded. About one in seven wounded soldiers died soon after from the wounds.

By December of that year, Walker moved to a field hospital in Falmouth, across the river from Fredericksburg, Virginia. Over 13,000 Union soldiers died, sustained wounds, or went missing in the Battle of Fredericksburg, which they lost.

Walker's next appointment, and her last as only a volunteer, was in Chattanooga, Tennessee. The Battle of Chickamauga took place from September 18 to 20, 1863. Here, the Union army attempted to strengthen its control of the city of Chattanooga but was defeated. This "glorious Southern victory" resulted in the second-highest number of casualties in the war, surpassed only by the Battle of Gettysburg. Technically the Confederates were the victors of this battle, but although they surrounded the city of Chattanooga, Union men remained within until November. Walker was among them and helped the wounded soldiers. The city was cold and vermin infested, with very few

The Battle of Chattanooga, fought shortly after the Battle of Chickamauga, was a Union victory and afforded Grant control of Tennessee.

resources due to the Confederate blockades, and was under constant siege by Southern forces. It was here that Walker met General George H. Thomas, who recommended Walker for her first position as a paid contractor with the army.

Employed at Last

Walker became the acting assistant surgeon, a civilian contract surgeon, with the Fifty-Second Ohio Volunteers stationed at Gordon's Mills, southeast of Chattanooga. However, when Walker arrived, the medical director of the Ohio troops, Dr. G. Perin, immediately took a disliking to her. He did not want his troops treated by Walker, whom he called a "medical monstrosity." He ordered that a medical board examine her qualifications. Thus, Walker had to endure an exam simply because Dr. Perin did not like her. It was quite clear that the in-person examination was basically a "kangaroo court," or a charade, conducted by male doctors looking for any reason to disqualify her.

In their report, the examiners stated that they doubted Walker had ever been to medical school, and they said she had no more medical knowledge than the average housewife. Even so, she was allowed to remain at her post. Unfortunately, this exam and the findings from it refused to stay in Walker's past: after the war, when Walker petitioned for her services to be recognized with a retroactive commission, one of the doctors who had been on the examination board submitted a letter of disapproval about her. This letter might have been the reason she was turned down. While the judge who had been tasked with the decision had many letters commending Walker, he still denied her petition.

Walker's time with the Fifty-Second Ohio did not coincide with a bloody battle, and the soldiers were in their winter quarters, in relatively good health. Having fewer crises to attend to with the soldiers, Walker regularly attended to the residents in the region, which was a Confederate one. She found that, like in many Southern towns, there was a great need in the area because many men and resources were taken away to focus on the war. By her accounts, many families were glad to have access to medical care, even if they had suspicions of her at first, being a Yankee who dressed strangely. A side effect of her altruism, however, was that some people—often the very soldiers and civilians she was treating—believed her to be a spy.

Political Prisoner

"You could get along without food or sleep longer than most persons, and hold up under hardships; indeed, you are adapted to emergencies, and would excel in any hospital or prison services." —S. R. Wells

When the Confederate sentries captured Walker on April 10, 1864, they transported her to a Confederate prison in Richmond with the intimidating name of Castle Thunder. Some historians write that the name was meant to scare people, but others write that some truly horrifying acts took place there. Historian Frances H. Casstevens writes that it was one of the most controversial prisons of both North and South during the war, with the most "desperate and dangerous characters within." At the helm of the operation was Captain George Washington Alexander, who had himself escaped from a Union prison, Fort McHenry in Baltimore.

Joseph Ferguson, a Union prisoner of war, wrote extensively about his experiences in Southern prisons, and his writings were published posthumously in 1865. At Castle Thunder, he wrote quite dramatically, prisoners were often "handcuffed, maimed, tortured, hung and shot, whipped until the weary soul winged its way to the creator." The building no longer exists, and it's not certain how accurate Ferguson's writings are, but we do know that prisoners were executed in the yard and sometimes tortured. After many complaints that prisoners were receiving unduly harsh treatments the Confederate House of Representatives launched an investigation into the prison during the war. The investigation cleared Alexander of all charges in 1863. It is dubious how rigorous an investigation

Part of the exterior of Castle Thunder, or as Walker called it, Hotel de Castle Thunder

into its own prison system a government could be, when the prison mostly existed to punish and detain their very enemies.

Many prisoners attempted to escape from Castle Thunder. About as many were successful as not. Prisoners took to tearing up blankets and making ropes out of them, plotting escapes out of windows. It's estimated that about one-third of all the blankets at Castle Thunder became ropes in this fashion.

The prison population was diverse, but the main charges included spying, deserting, and disloyalty. Sometimes it exceeded its capacity of 1,400 prisoners. For this, there was an extra building across the road called—perhaps humorously—Castle Lightning. Walker was one of about 100 women that the prison held during the war.

Shortly after arriving in prison, Walker wrote a letter to her parents, reassuring them that she was in good care: "I hope you are not grieving about me because I am a prisoner of war. I am living in a three-story brick 'castle' with plenty to eat, and a clean bed to sleep in. I have a roommate, a young lady about twenty years of age from near Corinth, Mississippi … The officers are gentlemanly and kind, and it will not be long before I am exchanged."

Walker also joked about her imprisonment afterward, calling the place "Hotel de Castle Thunder." However, with passing years, she later related grislier details, like terrible food and vermin. She also wrote that she spoke with the provost marshal while imprisoned, and that he told her that he would be more sympathetic to her if she would only dress like other women—Walker was, of course, wearing her reform dress as usual. She would not change her style of dress even if it gave her a chance of getting out of prison. She did, however, write many letters asking for her release. Her release via a prisoner swap came on August 12, 1864. The South exchanged her for a Confederate surgeon from Tennessee being held by the Union.

Since Walker gave so many varying descriptions of her treatment in the prison, it is hard to tell what she really underwent. Nevertheless, she did experience muscular atrophy during the four months, and she endured ongoing health issues. She had vision problems for the rest of her life, eventually impeding her ability to practice medicine.

From Prisoner to Prison Doctor

About a month after her release from Castle Thunder, Walker received an assignment (continuing as a civilian contractor) as surgeon in charge at the Women's Prison Hospital in Louisville, Kentucky. This was a Union institution. The inmates were female Confederates, some of whom had been accused of spying, much like Walker herself had been months before.

Coming out of prison and into this job, Walker basically walked from one hostile environment to another. Before her arrival, the surgeon in charge, Dr. Brown, was responsible for both male and female inmates. After Walker began the post, he was relegated to only the male population. He complained frequently of her "tyrannical" behavior. Other employees, as well as inmates, felt bothered by her presence and methods, and even lobbied for her removal.

Walker believed her job was to take care of the inmates' physical and moral well-being. From what is known about Walker's personality, she enjoyed and took pride in being so important to others. Yet, in Louisville, she was not in charge of Union soldiers but of Confederate prisoners. The inmates were not used to "such a watchful eye," as historian Elizabeth

D. Leonard puts it, and most likely distrusted Walker because she was a female authority figure and a Northerner to boot.

Only a month after Walker's arrival, the inmates penned a letter to Colonel Fairleigh, military commander of the Twenty-Sixth Kentucky Volunteers. They asked that he would "remove Dr. Walker as none of the inmates will receive her Medicine," and even suggested that he "give us another Surgeon, if not let us remain without any Surgeon." The military chain of command did not remove Walker from her post.

A few months later, in January, Walker complained of meeting resistance from the inmates. She had taken her job description to mean much more than medical responsibilities: she did not allow the inmates to sing Confederate songs or engage in "disloyal talk"; she replaced four of the male cooks with female ones; she monitored inmates' cleanliness and behavior; and she was not afraid to implement punishment for insubordination. Clearly, she enjoyed having authority as much as she enjoyed helping others. She outlined her concerns in a letter to Lieutenant Colonel Coyle, her post commandant. Instead of hearing back from Coyle, she heard from the assistant surgeon general's office, telling her: "You will exercise no other authority than that of a physician and inflict no punishments." She was ordered to keep her role strictly professional and simply medical.

Thus, Walker sustained criticism from her patients, subordinates, and superiors. Being at once a medical professional and an employee of the military, yet also not a full employee, and a woman, proved a challenge, of course. Walker employed the policy of asking for forgiveness rather than for permission, and she preferred to define her roles for herself. She cannot have appreciated others imposing restrictions on her.

In March of 1865, Walker requested to move from the prison hospital to a location more near the battlefront. She did receive a new assignment, but not near battle; she was assigned to an orphans' asylum in Clarksville, Tennessee. Most likely, Post Medical Director Phelps, whom she asked for her new assignment, did not want to kick up controversy again by placing Walker in the strategic position that she so desperately wanted. The orphanage was probably a more politically safe option.

In his iconic nine-part documentary on the Civil War, Ken Burns describes the residents of Clarksville as "prisoners in their own homes." Fort Defiance, located on a hilltop at the confluence of two rivers in the town, was a Confederate lookout and defense point until Union soldiers captured it and took over in February of 1862. Many towns, especially those somewhat between North and South, changed hands between Confederate and Union charge several times over the course of the war. Many families found their towns occupied by the same side that their brothers and sons were away fighting. Walker remained in Clarksville for only a number of weeks before Dr. George Cooper from the Medical Department came to relieve her.

Cooper carried a letter informing Walker that "your services are no longer required at this Dept." Shortly, on June 15, 1865, Walker's contract was officially terminated. While the war had lasted much longer than anyone initially expected, it had finally ended with General Lee's surrender in April.

Walker pursued a job as a peacetime doctor for the government, first as a medical inspector for the Bureau of Refugees and Freedmen. Many of the doctors who had worked with her throughout the war sent letters to President Andrew

Johnson, recommending "Miss Major Mary E. Walker," as they called her, for governmental employ. The Connecticut state agent for the Freedmen's Bureau even urged the president to appoint her. Aside from a job, Walker also requested a retroactive commission so that her services over the past years would be acknowledged. Even after the war was over, she did not relent in her quest to be recognized and referred to as a member—not simply a contractor—of the Union army.

However, President Johnson did not grant her requests. Judge Advocate General J. Holt of the War Department's Bureau of Military Justice, whom Johnson had tasked with synthesizing all the praise and condemnation of Walker that they had received, decided that "Miss Walker has not succeeded in satisfying the requirements of the medical department of the army." Once again, Walker's "unconventional" or "unsatisfactory" medical education worked against her. Likely, it was the easiest excuse for the government to justify not hiring her. Her wartime experience did not seem to factor in the final decision. The letter that informed Walker that her request would be denied stated, "There is no law or precedent which would authorize it."

Days later, President Johnson signed the bill that conferred the Congressional **Medal of Honor** for Meritorious Service upon Mary Walker. The medal was really a cover-up for, not a solution to, the adversity she had faced throughout the war, and the next chapter will touch on this in more detail. However, Walker did wear the medal every day until her death.

Dress Reform and Disturbances

In 1866, Walker's acquaintances at the *Sibyl*, a magazine dedicated to hydrotherapy and dress reform, asked her to take a prominent role in the dress reform movement, and she did. On a June day, Walker went shopping in New York City, wearing her usual reform garb, and was nearly arrested. While Walker was browsing in a millinery store, the shopkeeper called the police, worried that Walker was not safe, due to a large number of people following her around, staring, and making comments. When an officer arrived, Walker insisted that she needed no protection, referencing the medal on her chest. She at first refused to tell him her name or address when he asked. He then threatened to put her in jail if she did not cooperate, so she cooperated and wrote down his badge number. The officer offered to escort her home. "When I wish the protection of a policeman," Walker wittily replied, "I will ask an intelligent one."

Walker brought a case against the officer, filing charges of improper conduct. When the case came before the police commissioner a few days later, a crowd filled with people and press had gathered. Walker used this opportunity of testimony to get her message across, launching into an explanation of dress reform and showing no interest in returning to the topic of the police officer.

The judge concluded that she could wear what she wanted, as long as she did not create a disturbance. The police commissioner framed his argument as being about Walker's safety and not about creating a disturbance. The reactions from the public varied widely. Some newspapers latched on to Walker's dress and condemned it as immodest and improper.

Shortly after her court appearance, Walker attended the convention of the National Dress Reform Association. She was elected interim president and delivered a speech on the first

This photograph shows Walker after the war. Note the watch chain at her waist.

day. The speech mostly focused on the story of her near arrest but also included some predictions for the future. In ten years, Walker believed, women would be allowed to vote alongside men, as well as hold public office. Unfortunately, as she would later learn, it would take a few decades longer than that.

An Enigma Abroad

In the fall of 1866, Walker received an invitation to serve as a delegate to a social science congress in Manchester, England. She arrived a few weeks early and did some sightseeing in Scotland. Nearly immediately she amused the local press with her dress—she wore the reform dress regularly, as she had during the war. In England, people seemed to find it quirky and amusing, not the offensive choice that her fellow Americans believed it to be.

On October 8, she was introduced at the Social Science Congress as "a distinguished foreigner." In her talk, she covered many topics. She argued that Britain should give equal rights to its female citizens and spent some time addressing women's voting rights. One main concern of suffrage opponents was that women would just vote the way their husbands voted. Walker refuted this by saying that the wisdom of a vote does not depend on sex, but on intelligence. The content of her speech was not particularly original, but it did result in many invitations to speak at other occasions and to visit local hospitals.

Walker was invited to observe surgeries at the Royal Infirmary at Glasgow, at the Manchester Royal Infirmary, the Middlesex Hospital in London, and St. Bartholomew's Hospital in London. Women in the United States were not yet allowed to observe surgery. It gave Walker the opportunity to witness medicine being practiced with all the trappings of modern technology, in established hospitals, which were in stark contrast to the makeshift and war-starved locations she had previously served.

Walker's first lecture in England came on November 20 at St. James's Hall in London. It was titled "The Experiences of a Female Physician in College, in Private Practice, and in the Federal Army." The British public had been generally intrigued by the American Civil War, as well as alarmed at the number of casualties. A doctor who had been in the thick of it, who was also a woman who dressed in this peculiar way, made for an interesting headline. She found the audience to be somewhat disrespectful, with some unruly young men who did not keep quiet. However, the crowd also erupted into applause at certain points. "They asked me why I did not marry a doctor instead of setting up to be one myself," Walker told this audience, which garnered several laughs. She addressed the fact that some patients expected to pay her less than they would a male doctor. She retorted that her education had cost the same, her skills were the same, and she'd had to overcome higher obstacles—if anything, she should be charging more! But, she concluded, she would also accept "perfect equality."

The hour-and-a-half-long lecture was a mixed bag. The audience seemed most interested in details about the war experience, but Walker often brought the topic back around to dress reform, which was for her at the heart of many problems.

After this talk, Walker tailored her future lectures to focus on specific topics, such as dress reform (for a female audience), temperance (for workingmen's groups and temperance groups), and one about her experiences as a young doctor (for mixed audiences). One of her most popular topics was that of her imprisonment.

Medical audiences tended to be more critical of her. One critic wrote that she seemed in over her head, and that the result of her talk was "to throw ridicule on herself, her sex, her profession, and her country, and to strengthen the opinions of those who hold that women had better not meddle in physic." It was a vicious cycle, as some would say, that Walker's attempts to speak out and to make herself credible just convinced some people that she was out of her league.

Walker also made lecture trips around the North and Northwest parts of England, in Newcastle, Blyth, Durham, Sunderland, Leicester, Manchester, and Bristol. She also took a speaking tour of Scotland, speaking in Carlisle, Glasgow, Edinburgh, Kilmarnock, Dundee, Greenock, Ayr, and Hamilton. The lectures were mildly profitable for Walker, and she saved money by relying on the hospitality of her newly made friends. Since the start of her speaking in England, she had battled problems with her voice, and she endured coughing spasms on stage. By April of 1867, she had to decline further invitations to speak. She embarked instead on a trip to Paris.

In Paris, the Paris Exposition of 1867 was underway, and Walker attended some of the events, including a Fourth of July dinner for Americans. She showed up not only in her reform dress but with a sash designed like the American flag draped over herself. People got a kick out of this as well. She stayed in Europe for about a year.

Returning Stateside

Upon returning to the United States, Walker discovered that audiences were less hungry for her lectures than they had been abroad, which was not surprising since American audiences did not have the foreigners' fascination with the Civil War. In 1869, Mary attempted to tour the South giving lectures. She had a particular interest in reaching Southern women. "My heart is filled with *more* than *regard* for the Southern Sisterhood," she wrote, "for you like us must feel the degradation of all unfranchised women in a professed to be Republican Country." She received a mixed response.

In Kansas City, she was arrested for her manner of dress. She gave the policeman and the judge a piece of her mind, likely similar to how she had in New York. The *Kansas City Evening Bulletin* penned a short parody of the altercation in verse:

> Policeman, spare those pants,
> And don't make any row;
> In youth, they sheltered me,
> And I'll protect them now.

The people of New Orleans, which she visited shortly afterward, were not any more accepting of her fashion choices. She fell into yet another heated argument with an officer, and the officer threatened to imprison her if she was seen in such offensive dress again. Walker, of course, made no modifications to her wardrobe as a result of the warning.

The Complicated Path to the Vote

After she returned to the United States, when she was not traveling giving lectures, Walker based herself in Washington,

Suffragettes at the Republican National Convention in Chicago, 1920. The obscured word in the sign is "self."

DC, and dedicated herself to women's rights, occasionally practicing medicine as well. Unlike many of the suffragettes with whom she worked, she did not have a husband to help with expenses, so hers was not a life of excess. She lived for a time in a house with Belva Lockwood, who at the time was a dear friend and a fellow suffragette.

In 1870, Walker worked with the Central Women's Suffrage Bureau in DC, and she took a very direct approach to securing the vote for women. She and a group of other women petitioned that their names be registered as qualified voters in their respective districts. They then brought the petitions in person to the election officials, asking to be registered. The group arrived and marched into the marshal's office. Leading

Nurses and "Women's Work"

When she demanded official employment as a doctor, Mary Walker often shocked the male higher-ups in the military and often faced the suggestion that she become a nurse instead. In fact, more than three thousand women served as nurses in the Civil War. At least within the military, nursing was a relatively new occupation for women. Prior to the war, all army hospital jobs were men's, but once the war broke out, a much greater need for nurses arose.

Louisa May Alcott, best known as the author of the novel *Little Women*, served as a nurse at the Union Hotel Hospital in Washington, DC. She wrote of how the place was "cold, damp, dirty, full of vile odors from wounds, kitchens, wash rooms, stables." This was typical of most war hospitals, as they were set up hastily and housed too many patients. After six weeks, Alcott contracted typhoid and had to cut short her service so she could recover at home.

The Union army had such a great need for nurses that it appointed a superintendent of women nurses. This person was Dorothea Dix. She earned a reputation for being very strict about who could become a nurse: a woman had to be at least thirty years old and could not dress in the fashionable hoop skirts or wear jewelry. Many women quite resented working under her.

In the South, the taboo against female nurses was still alive. Being less organized and having fewer resources, the Confederate army did not have enough nurses in its employ but resisted hiring women. This did not stop Southern women, who took matters into their own hands. When a battle was being fought, families living nearby often opened their homes as makeshift hospitals. Sally Tompkins of Richmond set up a hospital in a friend's home with twenty-two beds, and when Jefferson Davis heard about it, he awarded her the rank of captain. Mary Walker, on the other hand, traveled to multiple battle sites, tending the wounded wherever she could, and never earned a military rank no matter how hard she tried.

Mary Ann Bickerdyke, a nurse from Cairo, Illinois, followed the Union army for four years and assisted during nineteen battles. The soldiers called her Mother Bickerdyke. While she had very little authority, she "charged through barriers," as she claimed that getting to the wounded men was more important than any red tape imposed. General Sherman gave her a high compliment: "She outranks me." Sherman was the same one who chastised Walker, once she had emerged from Castle Thunder, for her unusual clothing, and suggested that she try nursing.

Clara Barton was another notable nurse from the Civil War. She, unlike Mary Walker and Mother Bickerdyke, did not attempt to work within the system. Rather, she ran a one-woman supply operation and traveled with a carriage of food and supplies to battle sites. She was the first nurse on the scene at Antietam, and she wrote that she was so close to the fighting that a bullet pierced the hem of her dress. Barton was also the founder of the Red Cross.

We hear far less about women doctors, partly because there were so few. There was at least one female doctor besides Walker working at the time: Esther Hill Hawks, educated at the New England Female Medical College in Boston. When the government refused to hire her as a doctor, she applied to be a nurse, but Dorothea Dix refused to hire her as a nurse as well, likely because she was under thirty years old. In 1862, she became a teacher in Beaufort, South Carolina, where her husband, also a doctor, was working in a hospital. Eventually, she was able to work alongside him. They treated patients from the First South Carolina Volunteers, the first official black regiment in the Union army.

them was Belva Lockwood, Walker herself, Sara J. Spencer, Sarah P. Edson, Dr. Susan Edson, Dr. Caroline Winslow, and Josephine S. Griffin, and they were even joined by the ex-slave and orator Frederick Douglass.

The women approached the registrars and asked to be registered. The chairman responded that no, only males can vote. To the men, Walker responded, "As long as you tax women and deprive them of the right of franchise, you but make yourselves tyrants." She also challenged the idea that men are "protectors" of women, especially as they were the ones responsible for women's disenfranchisement. To this, one of the board members interjected, "You must marry a voter to get a protector." This episode made a splash in the press, and women in other communities repeated this **mass registration** strategy.

In the winter of 1871, a similar group involving Lockwood and Walker made a petition, gathering thirty-five thousand signatures, and brought it to Congress. They asked Congress to pass a declaratory act allowing women to vote along with black men, who were given the vote in the Fifteenth Amendment. While they did gain an audience with one member of Congress, they were not successful.

These two strategies, mass registration and the attempt to get Congress to pass a declaratory act, were the main tactics that the suffragettes had at their disposal. Walker was most fond of the mass registration idea, and even attempted to vote in Oswego Town in 1872. Many other women, including Susan B. Anthony, were participating in it as well, and sometimes they took their cases to court. Anthony, in fact, had managed to cast votes for state and congressional elections in Rochester. She incurred fines for this but never paid them.

Soon, after so many failed court cases resulting from mass registration, and after no movement from Congress, the suffragettes decided that a **constitutional amendment** was needed. Walker did not join up with this line of thinking. Because of this disagreement, she was not invited back to the inner circle of the suffragettes. She continued crusading in her own way.

In 1907, Walker wrote and circulated a pamphlet titled "Crowning Constitutional Argument." In it, she argued that women already *did* have the constitutional right to vote. She must have known that, literally, this was not true. In 1915, Walker attended the New York State Constitutional Convention in Albany, in hopes of blocking New York State's constitutional amendment that would have granted women the vote. Something she said at this convention illuminates her thinking: "I am opposed to granting men the right to vote on the *rights* of women. It is an unconstitutional usurpation of power."

Walker knew that the women's suffrage movement was pointing strongly in the direction of a constitutional amendment securing the vote for women. To Walker, this was like taking the wrong route to the right destination. It perfectly sums up Walker's strained relationship with others who wanted the same end goal that she did. She was willing to jeopardize, or even sabotage, the thing she wanted because of her principles, and the rift between her and other suffragettes widened over time.

Credit Where Credit Is Due

There was one more lifelong quest that Walker shouldered through all this. Much like she had spent her whole military career asking for a commission, she spent her veteran life asking for a better pension. Upon her discharge, she received $8.50 per month, but she believed that it should be more, especially when her partial muscular atrophy caused her pain in her eye and eventually required that she rest her eyes for long periods of time. Over the course of thirty years, starting in 1872, twenty bills were introduced in Congress that would benefit Walker and other veterans. In 1890, the Harrison presidential administration passed a law protecting veterans who could not perform physical labor. Finally, eight years after that, Walker secured a pension of $20 per month.

One of Walker's petitions to Congress for her pension is particularly noteworthy. In 1872, she was told that her petition was declined because of her style of dress. In response, Walker wrote up a draft of a resolution that, while it did not change anyone's mind, likely made them laugh. She offered that since the Constitution did not specify women's dress must be uncomfortable, foreign, or excessive, an amendment should be introduced to change this: "Whereas, an amendment to the constitution must be had in order to curtail a woman's right to relieve herself of the burden and undue expense of the covering considered essential in civilized nations," she wrote, "a national costumer for the women of the United States [shall] be selected from some foreign court whose special duties shall be to devise costumes for every woman." She further suggested that any woman who disregarded fashion plates should be punished by having her husband's pension taken away. According to Walker's proposal, the government should also send out a fashion magazine to every woman, free of expense.

The Minié Bullet and Amputations

The Civil War's main weapon was the **rifled musket**, meaning a musket with ridges in its barrel so that the bullet spirals as it leaves the gun. This technology was quite new at the time, and it meant that soldiers could shoot much more accurately, and from farther away. Claude-Étienne Minié's newly invented bullet, called the "minié bullet" or the "minié ball," was the main ammunition used in these guns. Previously, rifles were hardly used in combat because the bullet had to be forced down the barrel of the gun. Reloading with the minié bullet took much less time and effort, as it could just be dropped down the barrel.

Historians tend to agree that the Civil War was so bloody because the technology was way ahead of the tactics. Also, most of the fighting took place at very close range, 100 yards (91 meters) or closer. The doctors and nurses saw the results of this in the many wounded they treated. Since the bullets spun in a spiral-like fashion, they inflicted much more damage, often shattering bones. Doctors looked to amputation as the main solution when bullets landed in limbs because the bones seemed unsalvageable.

The Union army sustained about thirty thousand amputations during the war, with an average 26.3 percent mortality rate. The Confederacy is estimated to have sustained twenty-five thousand amputations. Anesthesia was available, but the concept of controlling infections through antiseptic methods was largely unknown. Hence the high

Union amputees

mortality rate, which can probably be attributed mostly to post-amputation infections.

Walker felt that surgeons amputated too liberally, and that in some cases the limb could be saved. This became yet another point of disagreement between her and other doctors. Often, to try to avoid unnecessary amputations, Walker would speak directly with the patients, encouraging them to resist by any means necessary. She must have learned confronting the other (male) doctors was fruitless and that she would not be taken seriously.

Mailroom Drama, or, Mary Does Not Take No for an Answer

After asking several people and procuring many letters of recommendation, Walker obtained a job as a clerk in the mailroom in the Pensions Office of the Department of the Interior in Washington, DC. This was in 1882, over ten years after her last steady paycheck. Relationships with her coworkers and superiors were unsteady. In a statement written ten months after Walker's start in the office, her boss, D. L. Gitt, maintained that Walker was "a firebrand in our midst, insulting to the ladies and inattentive to her duties as a clerk." He accused her of writing private letters, reading the newspaper, eating, and even sleeping while on the clock. Also, she missed 112 days in a single year.

Walker, in turn, complained of her eye problems, as well as pains in her chest and arms. In June 1883, she asked for five weeks of sick leave and received it. She also asked for a transfer to a different job within the Pension Division. Walker took off to Oswego, likely to visit her mother, and meanwhile was discharged. In her absence, Gitt had gotten the secretary of the interior to sign off on her dismissal.

When Walker found out about this, she went on the counterattack. After her sick leave, she showed up at work and was not admitted. She went to the office of W. W. Dudley, commissioner of the Pension Division, but did not find him there. She then went to his home that evening and would not leave until Dudley's wife finally convinced Walker that the commissioner was out of town.

Eventually, when Walker secured a meeting with Dudley, he accused her of laziness. Certainly, Walker's many absences from work were eyebrow-raising, but she could hardly be called lazy; her history, and even her many efforts to get Dudley's attention, certainly illustrate how industrious and driven she was. They had a two-hour conversation in which she defended herself, but at the end of it, Commissioner Dudley still recommended that she be terminated. Walker retaliated by revealing she had seen her boss, Mr. Gitt, having illicit meetings with a woman in the office during the early mornings. She even swore as much before a justice of the peace.

The secretary of the interior, H. M. Teller, probably thoroughly exhausted by this saga, passed the case up to the assistant attorney general, Joseph K. McCammon, for a decision. McCammon concluded that Walker had not been a victim of office mistreatment and that her termination should stand.

Walker took her case to President Chester Arthur, but there is no evidence that the president did anything for or against her. Having been ignored by the president, Walker next requested that she receive compensation for the months that these deliberations dragged on, July through November. This was declined. A year later, she requested that the case be reopened. This was declined as well, leaving Walker with no further avenues to explore.

Mary Walker, Sideshow Performer?

For some reason, either because she needed money or missed public speaking (or both), Walker took on a final series of lectures in 1887. Since she had no good connections in the suffrage movement anymore, she booked her talks with a firm called Kohl and Middleton. This series of talks represented a huge departure from her previous speaking engagements: she would be giving short lectures as part of sideshows at dime museums.

There seems to have been no point in Walker's public life at which she felt embarrassed or humiliated. Her sideshow gigs might have been the epitome of this apparent lack of shame. She gave short talks about her usual topics: dress, women's suffrage, labor, and tobacco. She refused to appear in any hall that had been poisoned by tobacco smoke. She appeared in Chicago, Cincinnati, Detroit, Buffalo, and possibly other cities. She did make good money during these travels: about $150 per week.

Later Engagements

In the 1880s, Walker started spending less time in DC and more time in Oswego. When Walker was forty-eight, her father passed away, and she began to spend more time at the family farm, taking care of it as well as her mother. At this time, Walker had also transitioned to dressing, for the most part, like a man. She wore a man's coat and pants, a stiff collar and tie, a silk top hat, and on occasion, a cape. Walker maintained she was not wearing men's clothes, but rather her own clothes.

Her increased time back on the farm did not stop her from remaining politically active. In 1881, she declared herself a candidate for the US Senate. As her qualifications, she noted that she had a brain that was not influenced by alcohol, tobacco, or other drugs. In 1890, she declared herself a candidate for Congress. Neither of these candidacies went very far. She also participated in local caucuses in Oswego, as well as state and national conventions.

Several quirky anecdotes survive from the later chapters of Walker's life. At the annual meeting of the New York State Historical Association, she met Franklin Delano Roosevelt, then the assistant secretary of the navy. She had no shame in telling him that she had not been fond of his cousin Theodore, but that she had a better feeling about him.

At the start of World War I, she sent a telegram to Kaiser Wilhelm, offering the use of her family farm as the location of a peace conference. He did not accept.

The last decade or so of her life must have been pleasurable for her: as World War I approached, Walker was no longer the only woman in pants! A brief bicycling craze at the turn of the century found popularity with both men and women. Since long skirts make biking very difficult, women began to bike in divided skirts. Bicycling would become less popular with the advent of Henry Ford's motorcar, but during the war, women began moving into the workforce in large numbers, so their wardrobe changed very quickly, depending on the line of work.

Walker lived to be eighty-six. She passed away in 1919, just one year before the Nineteenth Amendment finally gave women the right to vote.

four

Her Postwar Battles

*"You could go the world over,
acquiring knowledge and applying it
in all directions." —S. R. Wells*

Receiving the Medal of Honor may have felt like pacification to Walker, a condolence after being turned down for a commission so many times. However, she displayed great pride of the award and wore it daily. The medal was first awarded only a couple of years before Walker became a recipient. It was created during the Civil War to honor those

Opposite: Walker never sent her medal back when the government recalled it.

who showed "gallantry or intrepidity, at risk of life, above and beyond the call of duty."

In 1916, when Walker was in old age, a group of retired officers revised the army's requirements for Medal of Honor recipients, in accordance with an act of Congress requiring them to review the recipients. After their changes, 911 recipients of the medal had their awards revoked. Walker was one of them, possibly because she never engaged in direct combat with the enemy. She lobbied extensively for her medal to be reinstated, but the army did not change its mind during her lifetime. Walker refused to send her medals back—she had the original as well as one with a modified design from 1907.

In 1977, during the presidency of Jimmy Carter, Walker's medal was posthumously reinstated, and the official records corrected. Walker was one of only six people who had had their medal revoked to get it back, and it did not even happen during her lifetime.

Dress Reform, Her Dearest Cause

As has been mentioned, Walker believed deeply that women's clothes held women back from being able to accomplish more. For her, the issue was both a social and a medical one. Health had been more important to her than fashion, or looks, since the time of her childhood growing up with father's beliefs, until the day she died.

The average nineteenth-century woman's outfit consisted of a corset, or at least a tight bodice, with a floor-length skirt supported by several layers of petticoats. Corsets were made with whalebone to attain as narrow a waist as possible, the ideal being less than 20 inches (51 centimeters). Six to eight

A fashion plate illustrating traditional women's fashion in the 1860s. Note the tiny waists and large hoop skirts.

heavy petticoats were necessary to have a full skirt with that classic bell shape. Often, the fullness of the skirt was ensured with metal hoops, which caused the whole garment to sway awkwardly with any movement.

Reform dress, on the other hand, was much less restrictive. The top part did not consist of a corset. It was fitted, but not tight. Instead of reaching the floor, the skirt stopped below the knee, in the shin area, so that the pants were visible. The pants, or "Bloomers," were easily the most controversial part of the outfit, though dress reform advocates simply referred to the new way of dressing as "reform dress."

In her own use of the reform dress, Mary Walker received much criticism for creating a distraction or for being improper. It's evident from her own writings, including her contributions to the reformist periodical the *Sibyl* and her books, that she saw dress reform as a serious women's issue, not as a passing phase. First among her reasoning was health. Reform dress was popular among practitioners of water therapy. The water cure, as previously discussed, focused on exercise as well as diet and water-based treatments such as baths. Patients subscribing to a water therapy regimen often walked several miles a day. Water therapy itself was a bit of a passing phase in medical history, but it does stand to reason that if someone wants to have a full range of motion, and energy to move oneself through the world on foot, it must not help to have several pounds of clothing on the side of gravity.

Walker called the many layers of clothing a "sinful waste of time and energies," and wrote that it is "simply a matter of economy and duty" to have a better range of motion. Clothing, she felt, should contribute to, not hinder, one's abilities in everyday life.

Walker also believed that a person's physical well-being influenced his or her mental and emotional well-being. Women had been so overburdened with their outfits, she wrote, that "they could not cultivate the flowers of beauty in the garden of the soul, where the chilling winds of nervousness were constantly blowing away all beautiful sentiments." She also believed reform dress would benefit not only women, but men and children as well. If women could be healthy physically as well as mentally and emotionally, the benefits of this would extend to all their relationships, including marriage. "There can be no happiness without health."

Walker paid attention to all aspects of the outfit, not just the dress and pants underneath. She found the many accessories women were expected to wear on their heads

This drawing, showing Amelia Bloomer and others in the Bloomer outfit, emphasizes that it was conducive to outdoor activity.

totally unreasonable. She deplored the "extra braids, frizzes, curls, rats, mice, combs, pins, etc." that put extra weight on the head. Instead, she suggested that hair simply be worn down, so that it could move freely, or in a braid. Walker also designed an undergarment that she believed would be more comfortable and less likely to impede circulation as the usual tight stockings and corsets did. It was a one-piece suit with no elastics or bands. Her other reason for the undergarment was that she believed it might "discourage seduction and rape."

From all of this, it is clear that Walker wanted to make women's lives better, and she saw reform dress as a completely logical solution. "Nearly every roof covers a debilitated woman," she wrote, referring to the dress. "No one will, for a moment, harbor the idea that God intended such a solution." Of course, many disagreed. Some men, to put it simply, worried that women wearing trousers would make gender distinctions less clear and take masculinity and power away from men.

The "Bloomer costume" became synonymous with the feminist cause—a political statement, not just a practical, useful garment. Elizabeth Smith Miller, Elizabeth Cady Stanton, and Amelia Bloomer were among the first to wear it. These same women are most known for their work on women's suffrage. Susan B. Anthony tried wearing it but reported that when she did, people paid less attention to her words than to her clothes. Soon, the suffragettes decided that the reform dress distracted too much from their main message—the vote—and that the costs of wearing it outweighed the benefits. Walker, on the other hand, wore it regularly her whole life and, despite the fact that she did campaign for women's suffrage, wrote that "the want of the *ballot* is but a *toy* in comparison" to the importance of dress reform.

Unlike the suffragettes, Walker believed change had to start with the individual, and she did not want to compromise her values by casting off the reform dress. Sadly, the outfit had the effect of alienating people and served as fuel for those against the movement. It can be said that reform dress made it much more difficult for women's rights advocates—of all types—to gain widespread support.

A Scandalizing Author

Aside from her many lectures, Walker also wrote two books. The first, titled *Hit*, was published in 1871. It was dedicated to her parents, "the practical dress reformers," her "professional sisters," and to "that great sisterhood" of women. The mysteriously titled *Hit* has a separate chapter devoted to each of the issues that Walker advocated for the most: marriage and divorce, dress reform, suffrage, alcohol and tobacco, labor, and religion.

About marriage, Walker states it is a blessing and a joy. However, she goes on to say that true partnerships are rare, and one should not be bound, through restrictive divorce laws, to a husband lifelong. Courtship, the convention in which women had to be pursued by men, as well as women's inhibitive style of dress, were men's designs intended to keep women under their thumbs.

In the chapter entitled "Women's Franchise," Walker speaks at length on suffrage and the rights of women. She asserts that among other effects, political equality would lead to social equality, which could also transform marriage.

Alcohol and tobacco, which she staunchly opposed, were detrimental to health but also to the marriage relations according to Walker. In her book, Walker refers to the consumption of these substances by men, and the way that she believes it alters their relationships with their wives. "There is a lassitude, a general debility, a want of energy, an irritability, a defective memory; all of which are the results of the poisonous Tobacco," Walker declares. Her argument for temperance, or swearing off alcohol, is similar, as she describes the effect that it has on a man's wife and children: "At this hour wives and children are drinking cups of *agony*," while their husbands and fathers submit to the debilitating effects of alcohol consumption. Temperance organizations were big at the time, and soon after Walker's death, Prohibition would go into effect, banning the manufacture, distribution, and sale of alcohol. Prohibition lasted from 1920 to 1933 and, in fact, did not have the effects that temperance advocates expected. It ended up leading to higher crime rates, more unemployment, and more businesses having to shut down.

On work and labor, Walker argues that all professions are valid, and that both men and women should have the opportunity to learn trades and hold useful occupations, as well as receive equal pay. At the same time, she encourages men to take more of an active role in household duties.

In the chapter on religion, Walker states that the Golden Rule is the most important tenet to follow. She urges acceptance of different denominations of Christianity. A true religion "makes homes happy and ennobles life generally, by the precepts and examples of Christ." She resents how some had interpreted the scripture to mean that women must be slavishly subordinate to their husbands. Early in life, Walker identified most closely with Methodism, but later did not associate with it as much and declared herself to be a member of every church in a sense.

While Walker had many opinions on all different topics, most of her arguments circled back to women's rights and the ways that women could be better treated.

Walker's second book had an even more puzzling title and quite scandalized readers. *Unmasked; or, The Science of Immorality* came out in 1878. While Walker had aimed *Hit* at

The cover of Walker's first book, *Hit*

Detour

During Walker's time in the South, she received an invitation from a woman named Mary L. Reed to come to Port Gibson, Mississippi, and help organize a women's society for the promotion of women's rights. Reed said that the organization was prepared to pay her $600 for her counsel, $450 of which had already been raised. Walker replied that she would meet them on December 28, only a few weeks away. She immediately boarded a train and a steamship for Mississippi, and upon arrival, learned that the whole thing had been a hoax—Ms. Reed did not exist, and neither did the nascent women's group.

This experience, which had to be mortifying and costly for Walker, showed the opposition that she faced all the time. Not only did people ignore her or not take her seriously, but some apparently thought her a complete joke.

It remains unknown who instigated this trick on Walker, but she turned this detour on her trip through the South into an opportunity. She went on to visit Vicksburg, which had taken a particular beating during the later part of the war, during Grant's siege on the town. She gave talks there, as well as in Jackson, Mississippi. She then made her way to New Orleans, where she was nearly thrown in jail for her attire, as mentioned before.

a mixed audience, she wrote this second book specifically for men. The subtitle reads "To Gentlemen." In the introduction, she notes that many "private" treatises have been written by male doctors for female readers. Now that women are entering the medical field, Walker writes, it was only fair that a woman write a treatise for men. She saw it as her duty to enlighten men on many social and health-related issues, especially in their relationships with women. "It becomes the duty of whomsoever can peer into the darkness with a light, to do so with all speed, even if such light is no larger than a glow-worm," she remarks.

Walker was aware of the taboos of talking about certain intimate topics, but she saw the taboos of little importance when many women were suffering at the hands of men. "The arts and traps of seduction are talked over by men before boys," she states, "and so the youths grew up in the belief that there is something smart in taking advantage of women."

Unmasked contains a fascinating mix of arcane, bizarre beliefs and arguments, some of which were ahead of their time. The chapters cover such varied topics as hermaphrodites, kissing, men experiencing morning sickness, and barrenness. Citing her own medical experience, Walker explores how some men have experienced stomach pains during their wives' pregnancies. She theorizes that this phenomenon comes from "the wonderful fine magnetic intelligence through her nerves to his nerves." This sort of nerve telepathy came from "a power that is not yet fully understood," and could extend even to labor pains. These pains could be lessened, she suggests, by avoiding sexual activity during the pregnancy.

The chapter on kissing is truly perplexing. Kissing, according to Walker, can transmit venereal disease, and she believed that a large percentage of infant deaths were caused by

Dr. Lydia Sayer Hasbrouck and the *Sibyl*

Mary Edwards Walker and Dr. Lydia Sayer Hasbrouck (1827–1910) ran in many of the same circles. Both were lifelong advocates of dress reform, and both attended the New York Hygeio-Therapeutic College in New York City, although not at the same time. Hasbrouck began wearing the reform dress in 1849. After she was denied admission to the Seward Seminary in Florida, New York, for wearing it, she stuck to it as a matter of principle as well as convenience. It was Hasbrouck who later asked Walker to work with the Dress Reform Association in an official capacity after the war was over.

Hasbrouck, then Lydia Sayer, finished her brief coursework and spent about a year in Washington, DC, practicing medicine. In 1856, John Whitbeck Hasbrouck, editor of the *Whig Press*, asked her to participate in a lecture tour on dress reform. He also established a feminist periodical, the *Sibyl*, and Lydia became its editor. Just weeks after the first issue went to print, John and Lydia were married. They lived and ran the publication out of Middletown, New York. It ran from 1856 to 1864. Walker wrote columns for it occasionally.

The *Sibyl* called itself "A Semi-Monthly Journal of Eight Pages, Devoted to Reforms in Every Department of Life." Its focus, however, was dress reform, with some mentions of the importance of medical education for women, and the hydrotherapy that Lydia Hasbrouck practiced. With Hasbrouck herself authoring most of the journal's content, it had a dry and witty tone. Humorous poems appeared in its columns as well as

The masthead of the *Sibyl*, Lydia Sayer Hasbrouck's feminist publication.

letters from women readers across the country. One humorous poem about dress reform contains the following lines:

> Still may those who dare to be
> From all hoops and fetters free,
> Let the Tyrant Fashion see
> That they dare her frown.

> Sisters, if you wish to find
> Health and joy, and peace of mind,
> Bow no more at Fashion's shrine—
> Nature's laws obey.

The same issue contains a letter from a reader in Newburgh, New York, who wrote to Hasbrouck, saying, "I think you are not aware how extensively the short dress is worn in our city. Indeed, I was not aware of it myself, until we began to thaw out here." The contributor went on to detail the different variations of style that she had seen in the dresses, and to explain that men and boys did not, in fact, make fun of the wearers. She added that if the garments were starched enough, they did not even require ironing (a bonus, as the price of coal had risen).

Much like Walker, Lydia Hasbrouck was steadfast in her beliefs and not afraid to make a scene. In 1859, she refused to pay taxes on the grounds that she was not allowed to vote. When the tax collector stole a reform dress outfit from her home and threatened to sell it to cover the missing taxes, an editorial about him appeared in the *Sibyl*. This apparently caused him to drop the issue.

In 1880, New York passed a law that allowed women to vote for, and hold, an elected office in the arena of school offices. Hasbrouck was elected to the Middletown Board of Education, and thus became the first American woman to hold elected office.

parents kissing their babies. "The habit of kissing children is pernicious," she explains, and "the habit of general kissing is a reprehensible one since it leads to a greater familiarity." Walker is correct that kissing can spread germs, and in some cases diseases more dangerous than the common cold, but it is not nearly as big of a risk as she poses it to be. Her comment on familiarity, though, has more social significance: she expounds that the habit of greeting people with a kiss was unnecessary and often unwanted. Aside from the potential spread of germs, people should consider that a kiss may not always be welcome, and it should not always be given just out of habit or social expectation. When we assume, Walker says, we take advantage of people.

It was Walker's belief (and the belief of most people at the time) that sexual activities should be kept to a minimum, especially outside of marriage, and sometimes even within it. She states that it is important for men to take their wives' wants and feelings into account. Walker even provides anatomical descriptions to illustrate the physical pain that a woman might undergo in different situations. Sexual education is still debated today and continues to prove a difficult task. Walker was brave to take these early steps in *Unmasked* during a time when issues like abuse and sexual assault went largely untouched, and relations between husband and wife were not openly discussed.

five

Her Voice Echoes

*"You simply wish to be free, and to place your accountability between yourself and your Maker, rather than to man." —*S. R. Wells

I t is worth taking a brief look at the many issues that were close to Mary Walker's heart, and how some of them have evolved over time. It's no argument that women today have many more opportunities than they did in Walker's time—the 2016 presidential campaign, with a woman as a major party

Opposite: Today, women serve in the US military in greater proportions than ever.

nominee, being the most salient example—but inequality still abounds in some areas, for women as well as racial minorities.

Female Soldiers

As discussed, women were not allowed to serve in the US military at all during the Civil War. They could only help in an auxiliary capacity, as many nurses did, and never earned a rank. Since World War I, the armed forces have been opening up positions to women, but very gradually. A timeline of some of the most important changes follows:

- **1908:** Congress enacts language leading to the creation of the Navy Nurse Corps.

- **1918:** The secretary of the navy allows women to enroll in clerical duty.

- **1942:** The Naval Reserve becomes open to women. Also, the Women's Army Auxiliary Corps is created, with the stated purpose of "making available to the national defense when needed the knowledge, skill, and special training of the women of this Nation."

- **1948:** The Women's Armed Services Integration Act makes women a permanent part of military services but limits the proportion of enlisted women in the military to 2 percent and 10 percent for officers. The act is repealed in 1967.

- **1973:** Following the draft for the Vietnam War, the military still has difficulty recruiting enough qualified men, so more focus is put on recruiting women.

- **1979:** The Senate Armed Services Committee, when deciding whether to reinstitute Selective Service, recommends that women not be required to register for Selective Service, stating, "It is not in the best interest of our national defense."

- **1988:** The Department of Defense adopts a "risk rule," excluding women from noncombat units in which the risk of exposure to direct combat, to hostile fire, or to capture is equal to or greater than the risk faced by the combat units they are supporting. Women are also barred from combat jobs.

- **1992:** After renewed interest in making things more equal, legislation calls for a repeal of the limitations that did not allow women to serve on combat aircraft and naval vessels.

- **1994:** The Department of Defense lifts the 1988 "risk rule," but clarifies that women may not be assigned to units, below the brigade level, whose primary purpose is to engage in direct ground combat. This means that women still could not serve in the areas of infantry, artillery, armor, combat engineering, or special operations.

- **2009:** The Military Leadership Diversity Commission is formed. It conducts a study on the "establishment and maintenance of fair promotion and command opportunities for ethnic- and gender-specific members of the Armed Forces" above certain levels. Based on the findings, the Commission recommends that the Department of Defense should "take deliberate steps to open additional career fields and units involved in direct ground combat." This basically repeals the 1994 restrictions.

Women made up less than 1 percent of the armed forces until 1973, when the need during the Vietnam War led to more recruitment of women. By September 2011, women accounted for 14.5 percent of the active duty end strength.

The last areas that remained closed to women—ground combat, infantry, artillery, armor, combat engineering, and special forces—have finally opened up. In 2015, Defense Secretary Ashton Carter announced that starting in 2016, women would be eligible to serve in all combat roles. "There will be no exceptions," he said.

One division of the military did ask for exceptions, however. The Marine Corps—which has the smallest percentage of female soldiers, at 8 percent—conducted a year-long study that concluded that all-male units performed better, shot more accurately, and were more lethal than gender-integrated units. The Marines' request for exceptions was denied. As Secretary of the Navy Ray Mabus said, the study was based on averages, and the Marines should not be looking to employ "average" people as their soldiers, male or female.

As the number of female American soldiers grows, the military will need to make changes so that it is a more accommodating place for women to work. Everything from having uniforms made to fit women's bodies to having systems in place for maternity leave is necessary. Also, while the overall percentage of female soldiers is small, the number of female soldiers in higher ranks is much smaller. There are so few high-ranking women in the military that many potential recruits may not consider a military career.

In an admittedly older survey on sexual harassment by the Department of Defense, from 1988, 52 percent of female soldiers and 9 percent of male soldiers responded that they had experienced treatment that they classified as sexual harassment. While the numbers have gone down slightly in the intervening years, this is clearly a systemic problem that has festered due to the military having been a male institution for centuries. To make matters worse, 42 percent of women and 21 percent of men surveyed said that they feared adverse consequences if they reported the incident.

Equal Work, Equal Pay

We frequently hear that women make less money than men for the same work. The figure most often associated with the **gender pay gap** is around seventy-seven cents on the dollar. This seems quite an alarming figure, but how is it calculated? Taken at face value it sounds like a woman and a man, working alongside each other in the same job, with the same experience, would be earning different paychecks due to discrimination. Certainly, Mary Walker faced this problem starkly when patients felt she should earn less than a male

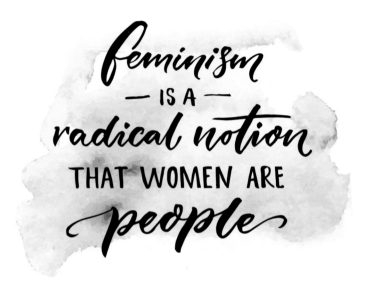

Feminism is often simplified in catchy phrases like this one.

doctor. While discrimination is a big problem today, it cannot be so easily identified. Also, there are many more factors at play than pure discrimination.

The seventy-seven-cent figure is calculated as an average of all individuals in the labor force that are working full time, for the full year. However, at the beginning of their careers, women and men in the same job tend to make the same salaries. The wage gap starts to become visible after several years in the career. Much of this has to do with what economists call "temporal flexibility."

Temporal flexibility is the degree to which an employee can dictate his or her own schedule. Women tend to value temporal flexibility more than men, not just because they bear children but because they are often tasked with other care roles, such as helping out aging parents or stepping in with other unpredictable family matters. If a woman needs to switch to part-time or work from home for part of the week, she would need temporal flexibility. And in some jobs, temporal flexibility is more expensive than in others. People have referred to this as the "care penalty" or "mommy tax." Depending on the demands of the job, or on the management, a woman who is taking temporal flexibility might not be considered for higher-level work or for promotions because she might be perceived as less committed to the job. A large part of the wage gap can be attributed to the fact that women may choose to work fewer hours for these various responsibilities.

Aside from working fewer hours in a given year, or needing more flexibility, women tend to choose different jobs in the first place. A female lawyer may choose to work as a corporate consultant, for example, instead of at a high-powered firm that places lots of emphasis on long hours and dedication. Again, the wage gap can be presented as a result of choices that women make in their careers. Sometimes it is debatable whether one would really call them choices.

Additionally, there is the question of whether women are even getting hired in certain fields in the first place. In 2000, economists Claudia Goldin and Cecilia Rouse published a study that explored the question of sex bias in hiring. They realized that orchestral auditions were a great way to test for this bias.

Before the 1970s, when an orchestra had an open spot, the music directors would hand-pick several candidates to audition. The candidates were almost always male and usually the students of the directors' own colleagues. In the 1970s and

@MaryWalkerMD

It might be worth thinking about what life would be like for Mary Walker if she lived today instead. She spent much of her postwar life on lecture tours. Today, authors, comedians, bands, campaigning politicians and others still engage in tours to reach audiences in faraway places, but lecturing is not nearly so much a big deal today as it was in Walker's time. This can, for the most part, be attributed to the internet. If people today want to hear a song, they can look up almost any song and listen to it online. If they want to hear the president speak, they can just look up any speech and watch it. In Walker's time, though, the song or speech wouldn't be heard unless it was live and in person. Wherever she went, newspaper articles advertised and documented Walker's tours, and many people went to hear her speak, having heard only a little about her ideas, wanting to learn more.

Fortunately or not, Walker's appearances in some places were treated more like performances than forums to learn or discuss social change. One venue in the London suburb of Camberwell gave Walker strict orders not to leave the backstage area before her speech because if people saw her before they bought their tickets, they may be content to just have caught a glimpse of her and go home. Audiences were certainly intrigued by her dress, her story, and her way of carrying herself. That interest, though, ranged from respect and admiration on one end to scorn and laughter on the other.

Walker never seemed to mind what her audience thought, and this might have contributed even more to their puzzlement.

Of course, even today, nothing quite compares to seeing a live performance, reading, or speech. If Walker were alive today, she might have successful speaking tours anyway, despite the internet. She also might appear on a viral TED Talk or two. Given how much she enjoyed broadcasting her beliefs and opinions whether others wanted to listen or not, it's plausible to think that she might have had an entertaining and fiery Twitter feed.

1980s, this process became democratized, and auditions were advertised to musicians' unions. Qualified musicians started showing up to auditions in greater numbers. On top of this, though, the orchestras began to implement another element: the screen, or blind, that would separate the auditioning musician from the panel of judges. Each musician would perform his or her audition behind the screen. The judges would then make their choice based only on the sound, without knowing the identity of the applicant. They would recommend that this applicant advance to the next round of auditioning or not. This process is known as "blind auditioning."

Over the years after the major orchestras started to hold blind auditions, orchestras became more and more balanced between male and female players. By examining rosters and audition records, Goldin and Rouse found that "the switch to blind auditions can explain about one-third of the increase in the proportion female among new hires." Another one-third, they wrote, was thanks to "the increased pool of female candidates." This means that not only were judging committees more likely to advance a healthy mix of males and females when they did not know the candidates' identities, but also that the change in audition practices encouraged more women musicians to audition in the first place.

Voting Rights

Voting discrimination did not end in 1920 with the passing of the Nineteenth Amendment. President Lyndon Johnson signed the **Voting Rights Act** into law in 1965. African Americans in the South faced many obstructions when trying to vote or register to vote. Some states imposed literacy tests, poll taxes,

Citizens line up to cast their votes in Portland, Maine.

and other bureaucratic restrictions. Many citizens also faced harassment or physical violence. Because of this, very few black citizens even registered to vote and had little voice in elections. Citizen demonstrations, as well as the attacks by state troopers on the marchers in Selma, Alabama, gained national attention and led to the passing of the act.

The Voting Rights Act outlawed literacy tests, and it appointed federal examiners to some districts who could register qualified citizens. It also required local governments to obtain "preclearance" whenever they wanted to make changes to voting practices and procedures. Parts of the act echo the sound of the Fifteenth Amendment, and the overall point of the act was to prohibit any restriction of voting on the basis of race or color.

By the end of 1965, a quarter of a million new black voters had registered. The act has come under criticism many times since 1965, and unfortunately, voters in many areas still face roadblocks when trying to exercise their constitutional right.

In recent years, some legislators have passed, or tried to pass, laws that make it harder to register and vote. Changes to voting rules make a big difference in voter and election turnout. Civil rights advocates have called these laws violations of the Voting Rights Act.

For example, in Texas's voter ID law, passed in 2011, concealed weapons permits were an acceptable form of voter ID, but student ID cards were not. A federal district court accused the Republican-dominated Texas government of creating racially motivated laws, creating obstacles for people who might not vote for the Republican political party.

The Supreme Court has shown precedent for striking down laws that are racially motivated, but not those that are partisan in nature. In many places, such as the American South today, there is overlap between racial and partisan motivations. For instance, most Southern blacks vote Democrat, and most Southern whites vote Republican. No matter what the motivation, whether it is partisan or racial, it should be illegal for a government to prevent citizens from voting.

People at risk for voter discrimination include racial minorities; Americans living in other countries, such as military personnel; people who have moved and therefore lost their voter registration; students; poor people; and convicted felons. Some states do not automatically restore voting rights for people who have finished their prison sentences. And four states, including Virginia, require felons to personally apply to the governor to get their vote back once they are out of prison. In August 2016, the governor of Virginia, Terry McAuliffe, restored the voting rights of thirteen thousand felons who had finished their sentences, bypassing the need for them to personally apply.

Dress Is Still Reforming Itself

The hoop skirts and petticoats of Mary Walker's early life were obsolete by her death. Dress reform quickly became a nonissue in the early twentieth century with the start of World War I. Fashions have of course changed since then, becoming more diverse and permissive. Are there any taboos that still exist? Do people dress today in a way that is detrimental to their health? Is there still some truth to Walker's belief that restrictive dress keeps people from "cultivat[ing] the flowers of beauty in the garden of the soul"?

Walker's Legacies

Walker was not right about everything. She believed that tuberculosis was not contagious. She was not in favor of vaccinations for smallpox. In fact, while in prison in Castle Thunder, she was offered a smallpox vaccination but turned it down. She recommended the use of onions as a deterrent instead. She encouraged many soldiers not to have their limbs amputated, even when the bones were shattered and

Women in Surgery

The field of surgery has advanced in more ways than can be effectively described here. However, suffice it to say that it has come a long way since the Civil War. Thanks to the rise of safer anesthesia and effective antiseptics, it is less dangerous for patients. It is also a highly competitive field requiring years of study and dedication, much more than Walker or her colleagues completed.

Surgeons today tend to choose a specialty, such as cardiothoracic surgery or pediatrics. They also have to complete medical school and a residency at a hospital, which put together can take ten years or more. Given the high stakes of the trade, it makes sense that the path to becoming a professional is very demanding.

The Association of Women Surgeons, a nonprofit educational and professional organization for helping female surgeons, states that the percentage of general surgeons who are women has risen over the past few decades. In 1980, 10 percent of general surgeons were women; in 1995 the number rose to 21 percent, and in 2010, it was 40 percent. The AWS exists to help women surgeons who find the historically male field hostile at times. Women surgeons face many of the same problems that were mentioned earlier with the wage gap question: they may need maternity or family leave, or they may find themselves passed over for promotions or raises. The AWS also points out that women tend to occupy very small percentages of high-ranking jobs in medicine. The American

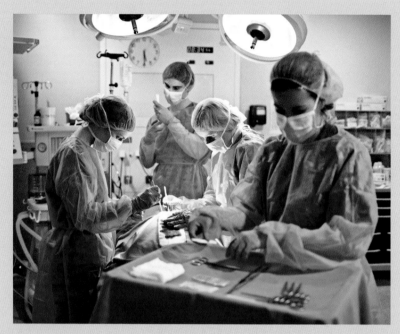

Becoming a surgeon today is much more difficult, but it is now a profession open to women.

College of Surgeons, an organization that is one hundred years old, has only had two woman presidents, for example, and only three female recipients of the Distinguished Service Award.

Walker dressed in suits as she got older. Note the rose pinned to her vest.

probably couldn't be healed with the available equipment. History can be quick to dismiss people who are sometimes wrong. Walker is not known for her skill or knowledge as a physician, but for her determination in believing that she was entitled to have a career and put it into practice.

Feminism today is very complicated, with many differing opinions on what will be most effective to enhance gender equality. We tend to look back on early feminism as simple— women fighting for their basic rights. Walker's story illustrates, however, that it was complicated back then, too. Even though she was not always successful, Walker's choice to continue crusading for her rights herself, rather than entreat the male sex to give them to her, is inspiring. The fact that so many of her enemies, as well as her former friends, sometimes treated her like a joke is very disheartening, as is the fact that her name often does not come up among those whom we have to thank for our rights today.

Suffragette Lucretia Mott said that Walker sought not to "act the man" but to become "the true woman." Today's feminism is interested in calling into question our very definitions of man and woman, and whether those definitions are even sufficient or helpful. Today's feminism may also bring new ways of looking at a historical figure such as Walker. For example, Walker shows up in an encyclopedia of lesbian, gay, bisexual and transgendered history, and is referred to as "most probably the best known cross-dressing woman from her era." Yet it may not be accurate to use the term "cross-dressing" in her case. Walker would likely say that she was dressing in the way that made her feel the most like herself. Today, at least in the United States, more people are free to be themselves than ever. Some still face ridicule the way Walker did for wearing her reform dress and, later, suits.

She might be left out of popular memory because she didn't fit into people's expectations at the time, and even by modern standards, she could be considered unusual. Walker

A photo of Walker in 1912

was exceedingly proud. She advocated for herself, demanding back pay and better disability pay for her time with the military. When her repeated requests for a commission were turned down during the war, she asked for a retroactive one after the war. When she received the Medal of Honor instead, she wore it every day. She refused to accept no for an answer, never gave up, and never compromised. Her sharp mind and demanding nature were not characteristics expected, and definitely not accepted, in a woman. Even today, women are encouraged to put their needs second to others, and to exhibit modesty.

There are several photographs of Walker as an older woman, dressed in her full regalia: pants, coat with tails, watch chains draping over her vest, and a white-gloved hand tipping her Lincoln-like silk hat. Her Medal of Honor sits on the left side of her jacket, and inexplicably, someone has placed a rose in her vest. In these photographs, she looks the most content, with a slight, proud smile on her face. There is also a photograph of her walking down the sidewalk in Oswego, going to her office, when she was in her eighties. At this point, she could not have still been practicing medicine, so the purpose of this particular office is unclear, but she always derived a great deal of pleasure from leaving the house, looking her best, and living her principles.

Glossary

abolition The act or action of ending a practice, such as ending slavery and freeing slaves.

casualty A military word that can refer to a death or injury in battle.

commission In the US military, commissioned officers are those who start in positions of leadership, often specialists in their field.

Confederacy The Southern part of the country during the Civil War, composed of states that wanted to secede from the country. They wanted a decentralized government, and in some cases, for slavery to continue to be legal.

constitutional amendment A change to the Constitution. In the US government, an amendment may be proposed by a two-thirds vote in both the Senate and the House of Representatives, or by a constitutional convention called for by two-thirds of the state legislatures.

dress reform The movement that advocated for the empowerment of women through more comfortable, practical, and healthy clothing. It was often seen as a passing trend among suffragettes.

eclecticism A medical school of thought that combined several other non-mainstream medical sects of the day. It emphasized preventative care, diet, exercise, and avoiding severe treatments whenever possible.

gender pay gap The difference in how much men and women get paid for the same jobs. It has narrowed over the years, but still exists, partly because of women generally working fewer hours, lack of equal opportunity, discrimination, or a combination of these.

hydrotherapy Also called water therapy and sometimes hydropathy, this was a popular yet not mainstream form of medical treatment in the mid-1800s. It emphasized treatments involving water, such as baths, as well as exercise and comfortable clothing.

mass registration In the few decades before women gained suffrage, some brave activists tried to affect change by simply showing up at the polls or registration places and trying to exercise the right that they didn't yet have.

Medal of Honor An award that was instated in December 1861 intended for recognizing valor in action against an enemy force.

millenarianism One type of religious revivalism that became popular during the Second Great Awakening. Followers believed that the Second Coming of Christ was nigh, and therefore they had to gather as many followers as possible.

precedent Past patterns or events that are used to justify current decisions. Trail blazers like Mary Walker struggled for acceptance partly because there was no precedent for what they were trying to accomplish.

regiment A group of soldiers that stays together. In the Civil War, regiments were composed of men from the same geographical location.

rifled musket A long-barreled infantry gun that is outfitted with spiraled ridges on the inside of the barrel, causing the bullet to spiral as it leaves the gun.

sect A group that diverge from the mainstream. Often used for religious groups that splinter off by themselves, and in Walker's time, for medical philosophies.

suffrage The word has many recorded definitions, including help, approval, or general opinion. It also means the ability to cast a vote, and women's rights advocates took on the term, calling themselves suffragettes.

temperance The practice of self-restraint and moderation and, when it comes to alcohol, sobriety. The temperance movement helped lead to the failed experiment of Prohibition in the early twentieth century.

Union The Northern part of the country during the Civil War called themselves this because they were fighting against the secession of the Southern states.

utopianism Another type of religious revivalism whose followers took to secluding themselves from larger society and living by their own set of rules.

Voting Rights Act Signed into law by Lyndon B. Johnson in 1965 with the aim of curbing racially motivated obstacles to voting and registering to vote. Resulted with about a quarter of a million black citizens registering to vote before the year was out.

Chronology

1832 Mary Edwards Walker is born.

1848 First Women's Rights Convention at Seneca Falls.

1855 Walker receives her medical degree from Syracuse Medical College.

1861 The Civil War officially begins at Fort Sumter on April 12. Walker works at the Indiana Hospital in a patent office in Washington, DC, for about two months.

1862 Walker receives another medical degree, this one from New York Hygeio-Theraputic College. She travels to Virginia late in the year, first to Warrenton and later to Fredericksburg.

1863 President Lincoln signs the Emancipation Proclamation on January 1 following the Union victory at Antietam. Walker travels to Chattanooga in the fall and helps out after the Battle of Chickamauga.

1864 At the beginning of this year, Walker begins service as a civilian contractor with the Fifty-Second Ohio. She is held as a prisoner in Castle Thunder from April 10 until August 12.

1865 The Civil War officially ends when General Lee surrenders to General Grant at Appomattox Courthouse on April 9. Walker's contract with the army is terminated on June 15. She receives Medal of Honor in November.

1866 Walker is nearly arrested in New York City in June and uses her court case as a platform to argue for dress reform. She begins her year-long European travels in the fall.

1869 Walker is arrested in Kansas City for her dress, and later in New Orleans as well.

1871 Walker publishes *Hit*.

1878 Publishes *Unmasked: The Science of Immorality*.

1880 New York law allows women to vote for and hold elected *school* offices, leading to Lydia Sayer Hasbrouck becoming the first American woman to hold elected office.

1890 Walker finally receives a raise in her pension to twenty dollars per month, after decades of campaigning for it.

1916 Walker's medal is disqualified, along with 910 others.

1919 Walker dies in her hometown and is buried in her frock coat in the family plot.

1920 The Nineteenth Amendment to the Constitution finally gives women the right to vote.

1965 President Lyndon Johnson signs the Voting Rights Act into law.

1977 Walker's medal is reinstated.

Further Information

Books

Harness, Cheryl. *Mary Edwars Walker Wears the Pants: The True Story of the Doctor, Reformer, and Civil War Hero.* Park Ridge, IL: Albert Whitman & Company, 2013.

Havelin, Kate. *Hoopskirts, Union Blues, and Confederate Grays: Civil War Fashions from 1861 to 1865.* Dressing a Nation: The History of US Fashion. Minneapolis: Twenty-First Century Books, 2012

Leonard, Elizabeth D. *Yankee Women: Gender Battles in the Civil War.* New York: Norton, 1994.

Films

Burns, Ken. *The Civil War (Comme.* Arlington, VA: PBS, 1990.

Ken Burns's famous nine-part documentary provides an enjoyable and immersive way to learn about the Civil War. He uses mostly primary sources—photographs, journal entries, and letters—to show how real people at the time experienced the war.

Websites

Changing the Face of Medicine

https://cfmedicine.nlm.nih.gov

The National Library of Medicine hosted an exhibit showcasing American women physicians. The website contains many resources as well as educational activities for students who are aspiring doctors.

Congressional Medal of Honor Society

http://www.cmohs.org

This website run by the CMOH provides links to the history and recipients of the United States' highest award for valor to individuals in the Armed Forces.

The National Portrait Gallery Presents: CivilWar@Smithsonian

http://www.civilwar.si.edu/

Public access to the Smithsonian Institutions's extensive Civil War collections and archives, produced by the National Portrait Gallery.

Bibliography

Barkun, Michael. *Crucible of the Millennium: The Burned-Over District of New York in the 1840s.* Syracuse, NY: Syracuse University Press, 1986.

Burns, Ken. *The Civil War.* Arlington, VA: PBS, 1990.

Burrelli, David F. "Women in Combat: Issues for Congress," in *Women in Combat and the Armed Forces,* edited by Redmond F. Hunt and Vaughn W. Mills, 1–17. New York: Nova Science Publishers, 2012.

Casstevens, Frances H. *Out of the Mouth of Hell: Civil War Prisons and Escapes.* Jefferson, NC: McFarland, 2005.

Chang, Ina. *A Separate Battle: Women and the Civil War.* New York: Lodestar Books, 1991.

"Declaration of Sentiments." National Park Service. Accessed September 21, 2016. https://www.nps.gov/wori/learn/historyculture/declaration-of-sentiments.htm.

Dubner, Stephen J. "The True Story of the Gender Pay Gap." Produced by Greg Rosalsky. *Freakonomics Radio,* January 7, 2016. http://freakonomics.com/podcast/the-true-story-of-the-gender-pay-gap-a-new-freakonomics-radio-podcast.

"Ether and Chloroform." History.com. Accessed October 21, 2016. http://www.history.com/topics/ether-and-chloroform.

Ferguson, Joseph. *Life-Struggles in Rebel Prisons: A Record of the Sufferings, Escapes, Adventures and Starvation of the Union Prisoners.* Philadelphia, 1865. Sources in US History Online: Civil War. Gale. Accessed October 16, 2016. http://galenet.galegroup.com/servlet/CivilWar?af=RN&ae=O100048033&srchtp=a&ste=14.

Flannery, Michael A. *Civil War Pharmacy: A History of Drugs, Drug Supply and Provision, and Therapeutics for the Union and Confederacy.* New York: Pharmaceutical Products Press, 2004.

Franzen, Trisha. "Walker, Mary Edwards." In *Encyclopedia of Lesbian, Gay, Bisexual and Transgendered History in America*, edited by Marc Stein, 3: 253–254. Detroit: Charles Scribner's Sons, 2004.

Gross, Rachel E. "Women Can Now Serve in All Military Combat Roles." *Slate*, December 3, 2015. http://www.slate.com/blogs/the_slatest/2015/12/03/pentagon_women_can_serve_in_all_military_combat_roles.html.

James, Edward T., ed. *Notable American Women 1607–1950, A Biographical Dictionary.* Vol. 2. Cambridge, MA: Belknap Press, 1971.

Johnson, Critchfield. *History of Oswego County, New York.* Philadelphia: L.H. Everts & Co., 1877. Hathi Trust. http://hdl.handle.net/2027/loc.ark:/13960/t9183nh7f.

Kirkup, John. *A History of Limb Amputation.* London, UK: Springer, 2007. SpringerLink. DOI: 10.1007/978-1-84628-509-7.

Leonard, Elizabeth D. *Yankee Women: Gender Battles in the Civil War*. New York: Norton, 1994.

"Prohibition." History.com. Accessed October 23, 2016. http://www.history.com/topics/prohibition.

Sibyl 1, no. 17 (March 1, 1857). Lydia Sayer Hasbrouck Collection, Historical Society of the Town of Warwick. http://www.hrvh.org/cdm/ref/collection/hsw/id/43.

Snyder, Charles McCool. *Dr. Mary Walker, The Little Lady in Pants*. New York: Arno Press, 1974.

Spiegel, Allen D., and Peter B. Suskind. "Mary Edwards Walker, M.D.: A Feminist Physician a Century Ahead of Her Time." *Journal of Community Health* 21, no. 3 (June 1996): 211–235. http://search.proquest.com/docview/224047885?accountid=10920.

Walker, Mary E. *Hit*. New York: The American News Co., 1871.

Walker, Mary E. *Unmasked: The Science of Immorality*. Philadelphia: W. H. Boyd, 1878.

Watson, William. *Letters of a Civil War Surgeon,* Edited by Paul Fatout. West Lafayette, IN: Purdue University Press, 1996.

"Why AWS Is Important." Association of Women Surgeons. Accessed October 23, 2016. https://www.womensurgeons.org/about-us/why-aws-is-important.

"Voting Rights Act (1965)." OurDocuments.gov. Accessed October 23, 2016. https://ourdocuments.gov/doc. php?flash=true&doc=100.

Ziegler, Sarah L., and Gregory G. Gunderson. *Moving Beyond G.I. Jane: Women and the U.S. Military.* Lanham, MD: University Press of America, 2005.

Index

Page numbers in **boldface** are illustrations. Entries in **boldface** are glossary terms.

About the Author

Alison Gaines is working toward a master of fine arts in poetry at the University of Florida in Gainesville. She earned a bachelor's degree in creative writing from Knox College. She enjoys writing books for young readers, as well as poetry for all ages. Unlike Mary Walker, Alison took some time to warm up to pants, and she strictly wore dresses and tights until the turn of the twenty-first century. She is originally from Vancouver, Washington.